AMNESTY?

THE UNSETTLED QUESTION
OF VIETNAM

AMNESTY?

THE UNSETTLED QUESTION
OF VIETNAM

NOW!

Arlie Schardt, American Civil Liberties Union

NEVER!

William A. Rusher, National Review

IF...

Mark O. Hatfield, U.S. Senator (Rep.) Oregon

Sun River Press
The Two Continents Publishing Group

ʳ

959.70431
SAm6
85297
oct1973

Distributed through
The Two Continents Publishing Group, Ltd.
5 South Union Street
Lawrence, Massachusetts 01843

Library of Congress Catalog Card Number: 73-84396
ISBN: 0-8467-0000-X

Production by Planned Production

Manufactured in The United States of America

Acknowledgments

Mr. Schardt expresses deep appreciation to Henry Schwarzschild, whose encyclopedic knowledge of the subject helped frame the overall essay; to Paul Good, Jack Nelson, and Barbara Matusow for their diligent critical readings of the manuscript; to David Addlestone, for his expert advice on military justice; and to Julie, Karen, and Kristin Schardt for their weeks of help and patience which made the project possible in the first place.

Mr. Rusher expresses thanks to his secretary, Mrs. Kathi Cowan, for her patient assistance and encouragement.

Senator Hatfield expresses thanks to Wesley Michaelson and Keith Kennedy, members of his staff, for their research, counsel, and assistance.

AMNESTY?

AMNESTY?
NOW!

Arlie Schardt

I

The entire debate over whether or not to grant amnesty to those who resisted the Vietnam war is overshadowed by an enormous irony; to wit, amnesty has *already* been granted.

It has been granted to all those responsible for the Vietnam war in the first place—those whose faulty judgment began it, those whose refusal to admit a mistake led them to escalate it, and those who piled official lie upon official lie to justify its pointless continuation. All those thousands of men, the ones who brought about the entire tragedy, have already been granted amnesty.

Or to put it more accurately, they have granted themselves amnesty. For they are in a position to do that. Coming as they do from the ranks of the well-born and the well-educated, they are not expected to pay for their mistakes in the same way in which the victims of their mistakes are expected to pay. Instead they have mostly washed their hands of the entire affair, except for a few hawks who metamorphosed into doves during the latter years of the war.

But for the most part, these men who perpetrated the war are busy with other pursuits now. They are bank presidents, foundation heads, college professors and corporate officers. They are, in other words, still among the controllers of society. And in that reality comes a second irony. Some of them will again be in positions of public-opinion leadership as our society begins the process of determining the fates of at least 580,000 young Americans whose lives are being severely damaged by the decisions these men made.

This is not to say that these people who led us into Vietnam and kept us there for ten years should be punished. No one is asking for that.

But the reality is that America has finally removed her ground troops from a war whose only purpose, in the end, was to get back the prisoners taken during that war.

If no accounting is to be asked of those who brought about such a tragedy through decisions made in the light of all the experience and wisdom of their mature years, how can anyone seek punishment for young men who made a decision in their late teens, in a climate where the national attitude was completely divided, and where many leaders were publicly stressing that America was doing something very wrong?

Why should this one group of young men be singled out, alone, as the only persons to be punished, when they were the only ones who were forced to make the decision that all other Americans were able to avoid? Indeed, setting aside the fact that over half the population was exempted from facing this decision because it was female, and nearly all the rest was freed on the basis of age, the fact is that even among those males in the draft-eligible age group only a small percentage had to make any choice at all, because most young men were never in danger of being drafted.

Of all those potentially eligible during the war, *no more than 11.1 per cent* were actually inducted into the military. They were mostly those without luck or influence.*

There is, in fact, a much larger class of draft evaders than those now being penalized for their open resistance to the Vietnam war. It includes those who went to college and got deferred; those who became teachers, ministers or pro athletes and got deferred or delayed; and those who were able to remain in the National Guard and the Reserves (some have wondered what it is for which the Reserves are always being reserved?).

Although amnesty is certainly not new to America (it dates all the way back to George Washington and has been granted thirty-four times) it is understandably hard for many citizens— still raw from the bitterness of the debate over the war itself —to shift their mental gears in an entirely different direction.

One day they were being told we must defeat an enemy. Next day they are being asked to forget the actions of those who would not fight that enemy. It is hard for them to think of

---

*According to the Office of Information, U.S. Selective Service System, a total of 15,612,487 men were examined from January 1, 1965 through December 31, 1972. Of these, 1,727,608 were inducted.

amnesty as anything other than a post-facto encouragement to lawbreaking. It is equally hard for them to conceive of supporting those who have broken the law. To them, amnesty must sound like a radical trick.

II

It is hardly that. Millions of Americans, whose background easily qualifies them as part of that "Middle America" to which President Nixon continually pitched his "us against them" appeals, despised this war every bit as much as those resisters whom he repeatedly singled out as the scapegoats for everything that ails our nation.

There are a number of Middle American values, including a sense of duty and a respect for authority, which in no way mitigate against the idea of supporting amnesty.

Among them is a concept called "Christian charity," which to many people includes Sunday school teachings about brotherhood, our fellow man, and Christ helping the poor, turning the other cheek and blessing sinners.

We learned that these are among the traits which make America a great nation. We are so big, so strong and so right that we can turn the other cheek. This is exemplified by our tradition of trouncing enemy nations in wartime and then actually helping them to rebuild afterwards. In other words, Americans do not believe in destroying other people, or causing them to suffer needlessly.

Thus it has come as somewhat of a surprise that while we seek peace with our declared enemy, there are those among us who are unwilling to make peace with our own sons. And that President Nixon, who readily granted amnesty to Moscow and Peking, forgetting their sins and drinking toasts to their leaders, seems bent on punishing only that one group who refused to treat the war as a Communist menace in the first place.

Why, one might wonder, should it even be necessary to persuade people to support amnesty when, in light of all the

Middle American values we respect, amnesty would seem to be an act of Americanism in its finest sense.

One might also wonder if the more virulent opposition to amnesty is anything more than a temporary expression of bitterness and disillusionment that would naturally follow any war which a democratic country never understood or fully supported; or whether it is merely the predictable response of some people after their President repeatedly urges them to make a pariah class of one particular group, hoping such an act might somehow bring sense to what is otherwise senseless, and justification to what is otherwise unjustifiable.

In sum, is much of the opposition to amnesty just a passing reflection of some mean-spirited, short-term politics? If not, if America is ready to banish a vast number of her young men, we are in serious trouble. For this would be a sign that America —a nation which has always been the beneficial recipient of waves of dissenters from repressive societies—has changed so drastically that *we* are now the one forcing *our* dissenters into permanent exile. Such an attitude would mean we are a society so ill-at-ease with ourselves, so fearful of dissent, that we are turning to repression to hold ourselves together.

More likely, however, is the expectation that the immediate postwar mood of opposition to amnesty will shift, just as so many other attitudes are shifting with such dizzying speed in today's society, where the only constant is change.

Vietnam is obviously something most Americans would like to forget. Indeed, except for the relatively few whose lives were directly touched by the war through their or their loved ones' involvement with the military, Vietnam is already a memory fading fast from the minds of millions of Americans. Had it not been for President Nixon's almost obsessive reminders that draft resisters and deserters personify all our problems (he even inserted one in the middle of a televised speech on the 1973 meat crisis), the issue would already be much less controversial.

It is hard, understandably, for people who have lived all their lives with a basic respect for authority suddenly to be asked to think in terms of simply forgetting the acts of a whole class of persons who broke the law. But amnesty for those who broke the law for reasons of conscience is an entirely separate category. Those who resisted did so not out of hatred for America, as many critics have sought to portray them, but rather out of a disappointed love of country. They saw in Vietnam the betrayal of the very values for which America supposedly stands.

The Vietnam war, American chapter, lasted ten years, or one-twentieth of our national history. It was a tragic episode, but only an episode. Even President Nixon called it a "mistake." Where so many shared in the mistake, the episode should not be used to single out and punish just one group, the young men who said no.

They are, after all, the only ones who actually had to make a choice, who were finally forced to take the risks, and to act in a momentous and decisive way.

No one, really, is in a position to judge them.

III

Amnesty is much more than the law's forgiving or pardoning an offender. It is the law's "forgetting" of certain acts (cf. "amnesia"; the word itself stems from the Greek *amnestia,* meaning not remembering or intentional overlooking).

Amnesty is not a right. It is a discretionary act of a sovereign state. It is a decision not to prosecute a class of citizens who may be in conflict with the law for political reasons. In forgetting, amnesty does not consider guilt or innocence. It does not inquire whether a crime has been committed. Just as prosecutors have the discretion not to prosecute (and they exercise it every day, with no apparent undercutting of the effectiveness of the law), amnesty is a government's decision not to apply a law under certain circumstances. It is usually granted after there has been a change in the political climate which led to the alleged violations, when it is "deemed more expedient for the public welfare than prosecution and punishment."[1] Often used in the interest of social justice and reconciliation, it is the law's way of undoing what the law has done.

Unlike a pardon—which applies to an individual who has been tried and found guilty, and thus implies forgiveness rather than forgetting—amnesty relates to an entire class of people.

Various types of amnesties have been granted thirty-four times in the history of the United States, some by the President, others by the Congress. Amnesty has been used, according to Cornell Law Professor Harrop A. Freeman, "to erase treason, insurrection, attempted political overthrow, tax refusal, civil and racial strife, draft avoidance, army desertion, disloyalty and espionage, even bigamy, polygamy and murder, particularly when these are caused by a political-racial-religious claim of necessity."[2]

In the case of Vietnam, amnesty should be as broad and all-encompassing as possible. The American Civil Liberties Union policy on amnesty is representative of those of many of the dozens of groups coalescing into a nationwide pro-amnesty movement. The ACLU advocates that all those "who face or have suffered criminal or administrative penalties for non-violent acts of evasion or resistance to the draft or to the military or to the war . . . and have done so during the era of the War in Southeast Asia, should be granted a full, broad and unconditional amnesty."

In other words, amnesty should be granted for every non-violent offense related to military regulations during the Vietnam war. The only exception would be for those who committed crimes which would also be crimes if committed in civilian life.*

The result, as outlined in legislation such as that offered by Representatives Bella Abzug and Ronald Dellums, would be complete restoration of all civil, political and property rights to everyone who has been prosecuted for failing to comply with any requirement of military service during the time of the Indochina war. The same would apply to civilians who were arrested for nonviolent acts of protest against the war.

*Only 10 per cent of court-martial convictions during the Vietnam era were for offenses that would have been regarded as such in civilian life. See *American Report,* May 7, 1973.

Such an amnesty would require the granting of honorable discharges to the 450,000 veterans who were given less-than-honorable discharges for all sorts of nonviolent infractions of military regulations. It would also expunge all notation of such actions from the records of courts and law enforcement agencies, and would immunize resisters from later criminal prosecution for their Vietnam-era acts.

Vice President Agnew complained in a speech to the Veterans of Foreign Wars last year that the current demand for amnesty is unprecedented—one of the broadest and most unconditional ever. He was right.

The amnesty now being called for *is* unprecedented. But so was the war which necessitated it. It is only in the context of that war that the need for this amnesty can be fully evaluated, and the justification for it fully appreciated.

IV

Americans voted for peace in 1964. They didn't get it. Instead, Lyndon Johnson escalated the war.

Americans voted for peace again in 1968. They didn't get it. Instead, Richard Nixon dropped more bombs than any other leader in the entire history of the world.

Americans again voted for peace in 1972, and finally the United States pulled its ground troops out of Vietnam and proclaimed peace with honor.

Actually, the administration had little choice but to leave. Public opinion was overwhelmingly against the war. The Army was simply not performing. Desertions were at an all-time high, and drugs were neutralizing thousands of soldiers. Racism was taking its toll in the Navy as veritable mutinies began to break out. And finally, even in the Air Force, pilots high up in the safe, sanitary sky began to say "enough." A few of them wouldn't bomb anymore.

It was the protesters who led the way in stopping the war, although it took forever. They energized the national climate until, by 1972, 73 percent of those interviewed in a Gallup Poll said they wanted to get out. The only condition was that our prisoners be freed. Those who still supported the adventure (and they were hard to find) were reduced to rationalizing "My country, right or wrong."

It was a war that never really began, never really ended, and was never declared by Congress—although such a declaration is required by the Constitution of the United States. It was, in so many ways, an odd vehicle to select for teaching the world about the wonders of democracy.

In tiny South Vietnam alone, our bombers literally plowed an area the size of Massachusetts. As one journalist thought back over the years of shifting explanations for our presence in Vietnam, he noted that we bombed to defend the cause of freedom; then we bombed to protect the lives of American GIs; then we bombed to get back our prisoners. Finally, in Cambodia, we seemed to wind up bombing just out of habit.

While the bombing was the most shocking and broadly destructive aspect of our performance in Vietnam, it was nonetheless only one aspect. Some 1,763,000 persons were killed, including nearly 600,000 Vietnamese civilians.* Almost 900,-000 persons were made amputees.[3] More than 700,000 children were made orphans.[4] Over 10 million South Vietnamese, in a country of 18 million population, were at one time or another refugees,[5] completely uprooted and often penned up in ramshackle refugee camps after their homes, villages and belongings were destroyed.

The ecology of millions of acres was despoiled and the land's productivity, in that agrarian culture, rendered sterile. Fearsome new "antipersonnel" weapons were tested, shot at and dropped on both military and civilians, some so horrible they

---

*According to the U.S. Department of Defense, American losses were 45,937 in combat, 10,303 in noncombat. The National Interreligious Service Board for Religious Objectors tabulated military deaths of 184,089 South Vietnamese, 5,225 "other free world", and 927,692 North Vietnamese and Vietcong. The U.S. Senate Subcommittee on Refugees and Escapees estimates civilian deaths at 415,000 South Vietnamese and 185,000 North Vietnamese.

were rarely described to Americans at home. My Lai and other massacres of defenseless women and children began forcing their way into the American awareness, yet napalm was commonplace enough that the thought of children's skin sizzling like bacon apparently just gradually lost its impact to shock.

In seeking some meaning in all this devastation, and finding none, one can only conclude that the epitaph for this war will be the ringing phrase of the American Army officer who reported "We had to destroy the village in order to save it."

To a growing number of Americans, that village began to sound more and more like the entire nation of Vietnam. While destructiveness and suffering were emerging as the hallmarks of the war in Vietnam, the atmosphere at home in the United States—where draft-age young men were anxiously watching and waiting—deteriorated steadily.

Yale University psychiatrist Robert Jay Lifton, who studied the psychological impact of that unease (as well as the psychological benefits that would flow from amnesty) reported that "Whatever the psychological defenses call forth, and they are considerable, Americans can no longer avoid the sense of having fallen into evil." Lifton found the country "is deeply confused, but there is a feeling, vague but disturbing and widespread, that not only the GIs sent to Vietnam but the whole society is in serious moral peril."[6]

Much of that confusion resulted increasingly from the asking of the question of just who it was we were fighting, and why? That should be the most easily answerable of questions for any democratic government that cares to explain why it is sending its citizens off to war. But it wasn't answered then, and it still isn't today.

Revelations such as those in the Pentagon papers confirmed that America's leaders were lying to the people on a consistent and calculated basis in order to hold support for the war. The frustration felt by millions of Americans, the mixed feelings of love and shame for their country, were lucidly captured by *New York Times* columnist Anthony Lewis, when he wrote: "Americans have always believed that they had a responsive Government, and especially one sensitive to humane considerations. It is a strange sensation to find oneself believing that that Government is now on the side opposed to humanity and truth."[7]

Lewis recognized the "added torment" of many citizens, "the frustration at their inability over so many years to affect the policy of their government." The baffled desperation of millions of people who had voted, demonstrated, petitioned, written letters—only to find their President barricaded behind a wall of school buses, watching a TV football game while over one-third of a million people clamored outside for some answers —was exemplified by a letter written to Lewis from a nun in upstate New York. "This is my country and they are my bombers. But what can I do to stop them?"

The mood was expressed, too, in a letter to the *New York Times* from a puzzled immigrant, now a citizen, who could no longer understand or explain why America, which he had chosen for her freedom, could do these things;[8] and in a letter to the *Washington Post* from an Army Medical Corps captain, a Vietnam veteran still on active duty, which publicly expressed his deep shame over the pattern of official lying employed to cover up what he described as our slaughter of the innocent and the helpless in Vietnam.[9]

The sense of despair, of being deceived by one's own government, ranged all the way from the IBM executive and his wife who vowed they would quit their spacious Westchester County home and move to Canada if the war was still going when their three sons reached draft age, to the plumber from West Virginia, who had served with distinction during World War II in Africa and Italy, where he was seriously wounded, and for whom his Army days are still so vividly happy that he carries thirty-year-old pictures and ID cards in his wallet. He vows that he would do anything for Uncle Sam. Anything, that is, except allow his teenage son to enlist in "that damn-fool war in Vietnam."[10]

Those people, and millions like them, increasingly asked "Why?" And they began to protest. As the government became more secretive, and as more lies were uncovered, the protests grew, until they were unlike anything that had accompanied any previous American war. All this was not lost on the draft-age young men who awaited their summons in an atmosphere completely different from that as recent as World War II, their fathers' war. In that war, only a generation before, there was virtually no political dissent. Americans saw clear-cut, justifiable needs. They did not have to be lied to. Today the professional veterans' groups, populated by elderly and middle-aged men who served in another war amidst another atmosphere, now constitute much of the opposition to amnesty. But the "I-fought-why-can't-they?" syndrome is totally irrelevant now. There is simply no comparison between the two wars.

Unlike World War II, where the need for American involvement was clear to the entire population, the war in Vietnam never had a consistently stated purpose. No American lives were in jeopardy until we put them there. It was not fought to protect America, since the Vietcong were hardly about to paddle across the Pacific in little yellow lifeboats and invade our West Coast. Nor was it fought for the acquisition of territory or, as far as we know, to develop new economic empires.

There wasn't even any grudge to be settled with an ancient enemy, or an old tribal feud to wrap up, since we had nothing in common, no history of relationships, with the Indochinese. Thus Vietnam had none of the traditional excuses for which wars are fought. Its only purpose was to serve the abstract political needs of various heads of state.

Equally sad, Vietnam was proving to be the costliest war in our history, not only in terms of wasted money (which was bad enough, reaching daily sums so huge as to be incomprehensible)* but in terms of social cost. Just when real progress was being made on America's most serious problem, racism, the war came along. It diverted the efforts of socially concerned

---

*At its peak, the war was costing Americans $78 million per day, based on Department of Defense totals of $28.8 billion spent on Vietnam in 1969.

leaders who had been working together, and split them into factions. Critically needed programs for health, housing, education, ecology and transportation were pared or shelved, while vast scientific research resources that were needed to help solve these problems were diverted to perfecting products for death. Runaway inflation imposed terrible burdens upon those living on fixed incomes. The passion and divisiveness raised by the war caused still more harm—those special kinds of tragedies only now on the wane, personified by the 1968 Democratic Convention, Kent State and a series of police assaults on protestors all across the country.

Indeed, although it wasn't fully realized until America was practically out of Vietnam, the war almost cost Americans something even more basic: their right to a free and democratic political system. For in the name of "national security," the administration set out indiscriminately to crack down on anyone who diminished the government's war-justification propaganda by demonstrating that the Emperor was indeed wearing no clothes. It was a program whose parts amounted to a systematic effort to undermine the protections guaranteed by our Constitution and Bill of Rights.

It began with an attack on the press, designed to discredit any reporting that might be critical of the government, especially regarding war policy.

This dovetailed with efforts to weaken the Congress by ignoring, belittling, impounding or vetoing its work. And it dovetailed with efforts to weaken the courts through the appointments of sycophants and reactionaries.

The program included, among its ancillary parts:

• The use of United States Army personnel to spy on the constitutionally protected political activities of civilians.

• The declaration, by the Attorney General, that he could bug, wiretap and spy on anyone whom he, in his wisdom, deemed a security risk. And that he could do so without asking permission from any court.

• The use of tax-paid agents provocateur to incite violence or set off disturbances in connection with civil rights and antiwar activities, thus making the participants appear to be law-breakers.

- The first successful use of prior restraint in the history of the United States, forbidding in advance the publication of an article (the Pentagon papers) in a newspaper.
- Invocation of the constitutionally unheard-of (to this day) doctrine of "qualified martial law" as the means for effecting an illegal mass arrest of thousands of May Day antiwar demonstrators in Washington.
- The complete perversion of the grand jury system into a tool for political surveillance of protest groups.[8]
- The violation of bank secrecy protections to discover who gave money to antiwar causes.
- The spying on, and wiretapping of, various newsmen.

These antidemocratic actions climaxed in revelations that came to be known as the Watergate scandal. For the activities just cited—all done in the name of "national security"—had also been serving as the vehicle for what might best be described as the closest the United States has ever come to a coup d'etat. Information leaks had to be stopped, said the administration, without explaining how information about the war cover-up could be a threat to national security, when the opposing army itself was not.

In any case, national security became the excuse for the Watergate participants to embark on an astonishing scheme. It included:

- The burglarizing and bugging of the offices of the Democratic National Committee.
- Breaking, entering and burglarizing various other offices, including those of a psychiatrist and some lawyers.
- Forgery of State Department cables, with the intention of distorting the very history of the Vietnam war.
- Destruction of criminal evidence by the acting director of the FBI.
- Perjury in a federal criminal trial.
- A federal trial in which some defendants were paid off to plead guilty and remain silent.

- More wiretapping of newsmen, plus efforts to intimidate some regarded as "enemies."
- Attempts to blame the CIA for certain domestic political activities.
- Formation of a special administration squad of spies and buggers, comprising a virtual fourth branch of government, and operating completely outside any legal, congressional or judicial restraint.
- The offer of a high government post to a federal judge, while he was in the midst of presiding over the trial of Daniel Ellsberg, chief defendant in the Pentagon papers case.

If most of these law violations sound more as if they were committed in the name of political security than national security, that is understandable. For together, they comprised a grand scheme to control the presidential nominating process of the rival national political party and then obliterate, not defeat, that party in the election. No chances were to be taken on such old-fashioned niceties as open debate, free expression, an informed electorate or the will of the people.

"National security" had become the foundation for an authoritarianism that would be the envy of any of the countries we have lately fought (on the grounds that they are "antidemocratic"). Its top priority was to crush dissent, relying on the very police state tactics from which we were supposedly rescuing South Vietnam.

It was an attempted overthrow of the Constitution, exemplified by an informal slogan in the Department of Justice—"The Constitution is not a suicide pact." In other words, if it gets in your way, ignore it. The scheme was engineered not by alien forces, not by domestic or foreign Communists, but from within by high officials, many of whom had used anti-Communism as a key to gaining their power.

It was all done in the name of national security, invoked in the name of the Vietnam war. And in what name was the Vietnam war invoked? Therein lay the paradox, the very troubling and profound paradox, that led such a vast number of

Americans to ask with persistent and rising intensity—why were we in Vietnam?

V

The answer actually has its beginnings more than a quarter of a century ago, long before we were directly involved in Vietnam. It began with the raising of the spectre of the Communist menace, which finally grew to such enormous proportions that almost any action, on any subject, could be invoked in its name. It played on that odd paranoia which has afflicted many Americans since World War II, and which raises a nettlesome question: namely, what is it in our national makeup that causes us to be so insecure while at the same time we are the strongest and richest nation on earth? Are we destined never again to attain genuine national unity except through some negative incarnation of a new "threat" to our "security"? When will we rally once more to a generous, elevating call? (Amnesty, of course, offers the opportunity for a positive response to that question).

In any case, America learned the Communists were on the march, somewhere out there 10,000 miles away in a country we couldn't even find on our maps. And the national paranoia responded. It was nurtured by many souls, all of whom assured us that the enemy is in Moscow and Peking, and from there, everywhere. Undoubtedly the most enduring political career built on this foundation is that of Richard Nixon, who joined with many others in conditioning Americans for the knee-jerk anti-Communism that made it so easy for his predecessors in the White House to carry us into Vietnam. We needed only to be told that this trip was necessary to "contain China," and in we went.

While Richard Nixon was by no means solely responsible for the creation of such a simplistic good guy-bad guy syndrome in America's international relations (he did not even hold a political office during our first five years in Vietnam), he was nonetheless a championship practitioner of the art—and it was the singularity of this reputation which paradoxically worked against him when, as President, he sought to persuade Americans to support his war efforts. For the question wouldn't go away: What made it so necessary to spill our sons' blood against the Communists of North Vietnam when President Nixon was clicking champagne glasses with the Communists of Russia and China?

The answer—that there was no answer—was too painful for some to bear. For many, such grand-scale, ironic tragedy could only be endured through the sedation of humor. Nothing was more helpful to such people than the wit of persons like columnist Art Buchwald. Buchwald captured the irony of America's dilemma in columns like the one he wrote about Rip Van Winkle waking up to the shocking sight of the hammer and sickle flying above the Executive Office Building of the White House.

> "Don't get upset," I said. "It's just to honor Leonid Brezhnev's visit to the United States. He's the Secretary of the Communist Party in the Soviet Union and he's visiting the President. Don't you read the papers?"
>
> "I've been asleep for 20 years," the old man said. "Oh my God, Richard Nixon warned us this would happen."
>
> "You don't understand, old man. Nixon is the President and he's the one who is entertaining Brezhnev."
>
> "It couldn't be the same Nixon," the old man said adamantly. "The Nixon I knew sent Alger Hiss to jail for playing footsy with the Communists. In every political campaign he warned of the Red Menace. He fought the Communists while everyone was being duped by them. Nixon would never entertain one in his home."
>
> "Times have changed, sir."[9]

Louis Lusky, professor of constitutional law at Columbia University, examined the contradictions of America's anti-Communist syndrome in a more serious vein. Searching for consolation in the Vietnam tragedy, for something of value in the valueless expenditure of national material, morale and manly treasure, Lusky noted that in Vietnam we may have learned a lesson that will help us deal with future challenges in a more humane, more effective and less costly way: "The war has done much to liberate us from the fiction, so carefully nurtured by Sen. Joseph McCarthy and his latter-day disciples, that communism is a unitary, monolithic phenomenon comparable to a killing disease—leprosy, say, or tuberculosis—which we are honor bound to fight wherever we find it . . . "[10]

Some missed the consolation. Lusky's insight was too late, for example, to help Air Force Captain Edward A. Brudno, who tragically became the first American ex-prisoner of war to commit suicide after returning home. Among the problems that had overwhelmed the thirty-three-year-old pilot, who had endured seven-and-a-half long years as a POW, was one pointed out during his eulogy. Captain Brudno was bitter, said Rabbi David Jacobs, about improving relations between the United States and China. "He had gone to Vietnam and chosen the service to fight the Chinese threat, and saw them becoming our ally. It made him question his own role."[11]

Millions of Americans comprehended these contradictions, but their leaders kept trying to drown out individual voices of conscience with high-decibel bombing. It only increased the demand for an explanation of why we were in Vietnam.

So the protests grew, and more and more of those Americans most affected—our young men of draft age—decided on their own answer. They said no.

No administration was about to tolerate this. No one was going to be the first American President to lose a war. Besides, we had to get our prisoners back. This legitimate need (which could have been accomplished by ending the war) somehow translated itself into "winning" the war, with the idea that through such a "victory" Americans would forget, forgive and, most important, reelect.

The "us-against-them" mentality needed to be sharpened if patriotism was to continue to be coupled with support for the war. Protesters and resisters were the easy "them." There were times when the enemy seemed to be not the Communists we supposedly had to defeat in Vietnam, but American citizens who would not support that effort because no one would tell them why they should. The conflict pointed up a second lesson Professor Lusky felt we may have learned from Vietnam, that "a society such as ours, in which the people have the ultimate power of decision—however long the exercise of that power may be delayed—will tear itself apart if led into a war whose necessity cannot be made clear to all or nearly all the people."

The need to free our prisoners was steadily elevated to become the war's primary, often its only, purpose. An odd kind of morality was promoted wherein those trying to stop the killing were made to appear antihumanist, indifferent to the plight of the American prisoners of war. A propaganda campaign of unprecedented proportions sought to smother any other points of view seeking access to the public attention. Even so, small courageous voices still struggled through, reminding us.

Novelist Grace Paley wrote one day in early 1972:

> There's a good deal of sentiment and dreamy invention attached to the American prisoners of war in North Vietnam.
>
> Politicians and newsmen often talk as though these pilots had been kidnapped from a farm in Iowa or out of a canoe paddling the waterways of Minnesota. In reality, they were fliers shot down out of the North Vietnamese sky where they had no business to be; out of that blueness they were dumping death on the people, the villages and the fields. And none of these men had been forced into the job. They were not drafted, they volunteered. They were trained. Then, out of the American sanctuaries in Thailand, the carrier nests at sea, they rose, a covey of brilliant down-swoopers, high fliers to do their work. Each one of these men may have accomplished a half-dozen My Lais in any evening. [12]

The naive arrogance that leads many Americans to think that others should always tolerate what America does simply because it is done by Americans, and the consequent ability of many to shut out the consequences of American actions in Vietnam, were both major factors in enabling our government to keep us in Vietnam as long as it did. Both characteristics were concisely captured by Ms. Paley in recounting a dialogue she had with the wife of a POW, who had asked Ms. Paley why the Vietnamese insisted on keeping our pilots.

> I explained that they were considered war criminals who had come 10,000 miles to attack a tiny country in an undeclared and brutal war.
>
> She said, "Well, they're airmen. They're American officers."
>
> I told her about the villagers living in wet dark tunnels for years, shattered by pellets—seared by napalm— I told her only what my own eyes had seen, the miles of maniac craters.
>
> She said "Oh, Mrs. Paley, villages and people! My husband wouldn't do that."
>
> I held the phone for awhile in silence. I took a deep breath. Then I said: "Oh? Well, I guess it must have been someone else."

Still another factor that enabled us to slide so deeply into Vietnam is the militarism that is so very much a part of the American national character. When one realizes that every generation now alive in this country has experienced a major war—World War I, World War II, Korea and Vietnam—it is easy to understand why the *single most commonly shared experience* among American males is the experience of having been in the military. There are over 29,000,000 veterans alive today in the United States, plus 2,233,000 persons on active duty. This has created a machismo syndrome, a feeling that masculinity is somehow equatable with fighting and warmaking. It makes a significant percentage of citizens easy pickings for any politician who wants to justify some cause (Vietnam) by setting up a whipping boy (draft-dodgers, cowards) as an example of the kind of undesirable character who for some unpatriotic reason does not support that cause. Therefore it must be a good cause if it has opponents like that. The machismo syndrome is so thoroughly ingrained in the American psyche that it affects all sorts of astonishingly unrelated areas. In the spring of 1973, for example, during a debate on a program to provide legal services to the poor, the United States House of Representatives overwhelmingly passed an amendment that specifically forbade Legal Services attorneys from representing draft-dodgers or deserters.

No one can predict on what manner of dangerous, destructive or self-defeating courses our militarism could take us. But we might better understand the chilling depth of its grip by remembering a careful nationwide survey taken by three Harvard University researchers. Half the people questioned said they themselves would follow orders and shoot civilians and children in a My Lai situation. Equally haunting, two-thirds of the respondents said they thought most Americans would follow orders and shoot.[13]

Given today's superdestructive weapons technology, the continued influence of militarism on the scale that kept us in Vietnam for a full decade could, in any "next time," have grotesque consequences not just for our foe, but for all humanity.* Here again, though, Vietnam may have brought an unintended benefit. For while militarism is still a dominant influence upon the generations raised on World War II epics and John Wayne glamorizations, even the limited glimpses of Vietnam reality that came through on the home TV screens have rendered the old style of prewar propaganda less persuasive. This, combined with the first-hand experience of the 2,600,000 American soldiers who actually saw what was being done in Vietnam, and the widespread aversion to the war among millions of their peers (who demonstrated this aversion by pulling every legal, quasi-legal and illegal string in the book to avoid serving) took away a considerable portion of the magic of war's image. To use one measure there were, by comparison with World War II and Korea, virtually no commercial movies made about Viet-

---

*We are already the weapons merchant to the world, providing $10 billion annually in military assistance to nations on every continent.

nam, although Vietnam lasted longer than the other two wars combined. That much of militarism, at least, just wasn't box office anymore.

If the very fact of the Vietnam war itself helped interrupt the generation-to-generation passing along of the warmaking ethos, the contribution which amnesty will make will dwarf this initial breakthrough.

In addition, as historian Henry Steele Commager put it, "Is there not something to be said for putting the government on notice, as it were, that if it plunges the nation into another war like the one in Vietnam, it will once again be in for trouble?"[14]

VI

Thus amnesty, by forcing us to examine our militarism, raises an even larger question than a nation's conscience and the immediate fate of a large class of its sons. It raises the ultimate question of whether there are any limits on the power of the state to command men to kill and be killed. Leslie Dunbar, Executive Director of the Field Foundation, thinks that we, in our time, are being challenged to determine the limits for such commands. In a speech before the National Conference on Amnesty in Washington, D.C. on May 5, 1973, Dunbar confronted the issue.

> As a national state we have become a great killer. Behind all the words and elegant concepts—words such as national interest, containment, balance of power, peace with honor—stands the death of people. These are the euphemisms that purport to legitimate killing, at the state's will. We begin in actual fact to define ourselves in terms of whom it is held to be legitimate for us to kill. There will come a day when this conceit ends, or else a day when humanity ends. Somehow we have to escape from, or secede from, the national state system. Amnesty would be such a life-affirming measure of secession. It would signify a reversal of the now absolute prerogative of the state to intervene in young people's lives, and to

dominate them for its own purposes. The freedom of the state from all restraint leads necessarily to the devaluing of life, and to devaluing truth and all else that stands between power-holders and their free and unchecked actions.

When we talk about amnesty we are talking about the power to make war. This means grappling with what Dunbar aptly described as the most urgent dilemma of contemporary mankind. "It is that the state, whose pristine and primary purpose was to protect and preserve life, has become the chief menace to life, and indeed, to life's very survival on this earth."

Dunbar's observation about the right of the state to dominate its young people raises the interesting side question of why the amnesty debate has until now been seen as an essentially liberal versus conservative issue. Inasmuch as the heart of conservative doctrine involves resisting the efforts of the state to impose itself on the lives of its citizens, it can be expected that as the debate moves beyond the patriot versus traitor simplification, conservatives will join those supporting amnesty. Some of this would be only natural in light of the process of mind-changing already going on throughout the country regarding our military policies, and in light of the fact that as passions over the war continue to cool, resentment against those who refused to support it will also temper. But a pro-amnesty stance is also likely to begin attracting thoughtful conservatives. They will see its parallels, for example, to the issue of the peacetime draft, which both liberals and conservatives have long opposed on the ground that it is an unconscionable invasion by the state upon the civil liberties of the individual.

The Vietnam draft, and the Vietnam war itself, were no less an invasion, and for the very same reason: our government not only failed to demonstrate that a national emergency existed which justified such an invasion, but our Congress never even declared a state of war as required by the Constitution. Under such circumstances, those who refused to take part, or were punished for taking part in a way that did not please the military, can only be seen to have been resisting an illegal draft and an illegal war.

It is likely, indeed, that one day the unconstitutionality of the war will be acknowledged officially. This could not happen during the war itself because the courts avoided hearing cases which would have compelled them to make such a finding. This was both an unfortunate yet realistic approach for the courts to take, since history told them that to provoke any such High Noon showdown between themselves and the executive branch would only lead to a serious diminution of the prestige of the courts, and the authority of the law. In times like Vietnam, when the national administration is so absolutely committed to a course of action, it is simply not within the power of the courts to turn the tide of history. It is beyond even them to play that dominant a role in our national life. Their ruling would have been ignored, there would have been nothing they could do about it, and they knew it. President Lincoln, for example, once ignored a habeas corpus order signed by the Chief Justice during the Civil War. And then there was that memorable day when Andrew Jackson said of a ruling by Chief Justice Marshall, "Judge Marshall has made his decision; now let him enforce it."

Today, however, with American troops back home, cases are moving through the courts, brought by several legal arms of the ACLU, which eventually may result in the Vietnam war's being found unconstitutional. The chief argument against recent cases has been that the years of congressional appropriations granted for the war, and congressional extension of the draft, amounted to implicit authorization of the war.[15] This would seem to fly in the face of the fact that congressional rules prevent members from using authorization measures as the means for deciding substantive questions. More to the point, Article I of the Constitution says it is the Congress that shall have power to declare war. It never did so.

If and when the day finally comes when the courts find the Vietnam war unconstitutional, that decision may well settle the question of amnesty for everyone suffering legal consequences from an illegal war. It will at least create a de facto amnesty, a situation where it will be virtually impossible for the government to overcome the challenge of anyone claiming his punishment was imposed as the result of conditions caused by an unconstitutional war. But that day may be some time in the future. Meanwhile, hundreds of thousands of lives are being adversely affected, in varying degrees of severity. Those who said no to the war did so because it was a senseless, brutal, mean-spirited action completely unworthy of American ideals.

Such a war would have been just as wrong had Congress declared it. Indeed, it was so unprecedented, so completely outside all the laws, values and traditions developed throughout American history, that resistance to it really must be weighed in the realm of morality and conscience. None of the old rules applied to the conduct of this war, and none of the classic methods for evaluating the responsibilities between individuals and their governments can be applied, either. In short, this is the exception that makes the rule. It is also why the law provides for amnesty; because sometimes even the genius of our system of laws is not equal to the task. In a situation so overmastering, the act of forgetting becomes the only possible act of justice.

VII

For the past three years, except for a period in Canada, I've lived underground in America, cut off from my family and friends. It has meant drifting from one low-paying job to another, often going without food or shelter. Like thousands of AWOLs before me, I'll be court-martialed by a jury composed of career officers, sentenced to a military prison and finally, returned to civilian life with a bad discharge to insure that their punishment extends into the rest of my life . . .

—Army Medic Eddie Sowders*
June, 1973

*In the above statement, released through the nationwide amnesty organization SAFE RETURN, Sowders relates how he decided to "desert" the Army after having volunteered for a second tour of duty in Vietnam, in a war he once supported. Assigned to an evacuation hospital, he saw that "Many of these victims were Vietnamese civilians, mostly women and children hit by U.S. artillery and bombing. Many had been severely burned by napalm and white phosphorus; weapons used only by the U.S. What affected me most were the children. I watched many of them die from their terrible wounds; we 'saved' others —to be crippled or maimed for the rest of their lives."

To appreciate the enormity of any attempt to mete out justice in the wake of an illegal war, the number of people involved must be understood. At least 580,000 are suffering some sort of legal disability as a result of Vietnam. This does not include the untold thousands who never registered for the draft, the possible thousands more whose status is in limbo because of the inefficiencies of the Selective Service System, and the many thousands of civilian men and women arrested for taking part in peaceful protest activities. All would be covered by an unconditional amnesty. The military-related offenders break down into four broad categories:*

Draft refusers—At least 7,400 men have been convicted by federal courts for draft violations during the Vietnam era. In addition, 39,000 have been referred by Selective Service to the Department of Justice for prosecution, while indictments are pending for 5,700 more.

Deserters—A "significant segment of the armed forces (about 5 per cent of the Army and Marines) protested the war the best way they knew how—by leaving." The meaning of this becomes clearer, explains Robert Musil, associate secretary of the Central Committee For Conscientious Objectors, "if one considers that in 1971 in the Army alone, 79,000 soldiers, or nearly six full divisions, deserted."[16] The term "deserter" is actually an administrative convenience for purposes of classification. It refers to anyone who has been absent without leave (AWOL) for more than thirty days. The Pentagon reports a total of 495,689 cases of desertion from August, 1964 through December, 1972. Some 90 per cent of these returned to military control, either by apprehension or voluntarily. This leaves 32,718 officially still at large. Amnesty groups contend the figure is much larger.

It is a comment on Americans' evaluation of the Vietnam war that the number of soldiers who "voted with their feet" reached a rate of 7.3 per cent of all Army personnel at its high point in 1971. This was more than triple the highest desertion rate during the Korean war, notes Musil, and "was also much

---

*Compiled by ACLU Foundation Project on Amnesty, June, 1973, except where otherwise noted.

higher than any rate recorded for World War II, when a greater percentage of U.S. troops were in combat zones and there were no one-year rotations."

Many people react more viscerally against deserters than against any other class of resisters. They regard deserters as either criminals who fled to escape punishment for other crimes, or as cowards. Undoubtedly some did desert to escape punishment for other crimes, but those crimes would not be affected by amnesty. Offenders would have to face the legal consequences for those crimes. As for "cowards," many men walked out because they were ill, or in order to help wives or relatives who were ill or in trouble, or because they were actually conscientious objectors who had been illegally or improperly denied that classification. Many others served with distinction in combat until they became sickened by the senseless killing, and would take part no more.

Exiles—An estimated 37,000 to 40,000 war resisters, along with many wives and children, are living outside the United States in exile, mostly in Canada.

Less-than-honorable discharges—There are about 450,-000 Vietnam-era veterans with less-than-fully-honorable discharges. This is in many ways the most disturbing category of all, because thousands of these men commited no crimes whatsoever, not even in military terms. They were discharged because the military found it easier just to clear out "incompetents" than try to train them. Many, of course, should never have been inducted to begin with, but this was the military's fault, not theirs. For thousands more, who became victims of the drug abuse that was so endemic in Vietnam and elsewhere in the military, less-than-honorable discharges were an easy way for the military to rid itself of the problem.

More than 65 per cent of the less-than-fully-honorable discharges were given administratively, usually without a hearing. "Opportunities for hearings, where available, were often waived", says David Addlestone, director of the Lawyers Military Defense Committee of the ACLU Foundation. "This was sometimes due to lack of interest by military counsel, and sometimes due to other pressures, such as illegal pretrial confinement. The accused wanted to get out of jail, and he had the choice of accepting an undesirable discharge, or staying in jail and standing trial before a court-martial." Most accused got the message. It could be a long wait for that hearing. They chose to get out as quickly as possible, regardless of the consequences of such a discharge.

Yet everyone, no matter what his "offense," is penalized with varying degrees of disqualification from veterans' benefits, hospital benefits, civil service eligibility, licenses and employment. Indeed, even "honorable" discharges bear coded numbers which indicate to government agencies and prospective employers that the veteran was guilty of anything from drug abuse to bedwetting, apathy or "unsuitability."

There is a charge vague enough to fit (or not to fit) anyone the military wants to get rid of. In 1971, 1,000 persons were given general (administrative) discharges for something called "inaptitude." Another 4,000 were released for "apathy and defective attitude," and another 15,000 for "character and behavior disorders." Personnel can also be dismissed for disrespect, for homosexual *tendencies,* or for asserting their racial identity through such symbols as hair style, dress style or using the black power handshake.

Short of all these options, there is always Article 134 of the Uniform Code of Military Justice, which the military still uses although it has been declared unconstitutional by two different U.S. circuit courts of appeal. Article 134 includes the catch-all, "all conduct of a nature to bring discredit upon the armed forces," which is innocuous enough to cover literally anything anyone in authority wants it to.

In addition to the above categories, which comprise a minimum of 580,000 persons whose cases would have to be handled individually in any plan short of amnesty, another 550,000 were convicted by military courts of offenses which would rarely be crimes in a civilian context. Since there is undoubtedly some overlap here with the first four categories, no effort is made here to add these cases to the others. Yet regardless of the total, and regardless of the category, the same truth applies to all these men: they would not have been in the military but for an undeclared war and an illegal draft. Their records should therefore be cleared. The only way this can be accomplished without further discrimination is through a universal amnesty.

Discrimination not only afflicted these men by virtue of sex, age, and their economic-educational background, it also afflicted many because of their race. After entry on active duty, blacks were disproportionately placed in pretrial confinement. They were also disproportionately given less-than-honorable discharges, and they received stiffer sentences for the same offenses than did whites even of the same educational and IQ level.* Although blacks comprised about 13 per cent of the personnel in the Army, 46 per cent of all courts-martial during the Vietnam era involved nonwhites. Studies are replete with instances of black GIs being punished for the same acts which were ignored when committed by whites.

The various degrees of discrimination, racial and otherwise, constitute injustice enough to illuminate the need for amnesty. But even beyond this is still another important factor, the common denominator afflicting all those who carry the stigma of a less-than-honorable discharge: unless their records are purged through an amnesty, they will be punished for the rest of their lives, either for actions that were not crimes, or for actions that were not committed at all.

> At the present time, it is entirely possible for a young man of 18 years, with no prior record of involvement with school, juvenile or police authorities, to be discharged from the military against his wishes, with an undesirable discharge under other than honorable conditions, based solely on the unsworn statement of a confessed drug pusher who is not present at the hearing.[17]

*Findings of Department of Defense Task Force on the Administration of Military Justice in the Armed Forces, 1972.

A few case histories, drawn from the files of Joe Garcia, director of the city of Seattle's Division of Veterans Affairs, illustrate how men may become, in the eyes of the military, "less than honorable."

• A young Seattle man enlisted in the Air Force in 1969 at age eighteen. He had a high scholastic average and a clean disciplinary record. He had considered seeking conscientious objector status but was advised he was ineligible. After receiving the highest possible evaluation for his work as an Air Force accountant he learned that CO standards had been broadened, and sought to apply. He was told by his superior that COs were draft-dodgers and "should all be sent to Russia." His job-performance rating was soon found to be "unsatisfactory," and a psychiatrist seen in connection with his CO application labeled him an "immature personality." His room and person were searched for narcotics. None were found. On the basis of an unsubstantiated, unsworn statement of a confessed drug user, the young man was given an undesirable discharge after serving two years and three months.

• An eighteen-year-old enlisted in the Marines. After only twenty-four days, he was given a general discharge. He had no police record and no Marine Corps disciplinary action was pending. He was administratively discharged, according to the record, because his "long history of emotional inconsistency" meant that "he enlisted in bad faith." He was deemed "an immature, confused, mixed up and sorry individual. He stutters and stammers and it is difficult for him to express himself coherently. His best efforts will never be enough to get him through recruit training." It was apparently a mistake for the Marines to sign up a youngster with so many emotional problems. But it is the young man, not the Marines, who is paying for the Marines' mistake.

• A seventeen-year-old enlisted in the Army Airborne Infantry. Describing himself as "patriotic as hell," he had served eleven months as a combat medic in Vietnam when he was hit by a grenade and hospitalized in the United States. The medic who took his place, a close buddy, was killed twenty minutes after replacing him. Released to Ft. Lewis, Washington, after his hospital discharge, he became depressed and began drinking heavily. Once he went AWOL for twenty-three days. After an attempted suicide, he was committed to a hospital and treated for acute alcoholism. Upon returning to Ft. Lewis, he was ordered immediately into the stockade, where he spent thirty days. He was then given a summary court martial and administratively discharged as an undesirable. His discharge came exactly one month before termination of his three-year enlistment.

Only through amnesty, which will expunge servicemen's records of all nonviolent, Vietnam-era charges, can the continuing punishment of these and at least a half-million other men finally be ended. This is an especially vital obligation today, for we live in what Aryeh Neier describes as a "records prison,"[18] in which dossiers of information about our personal lives —credit records, arrest records, driving, banking and marital records—follow us wherever we go. Although many dossiers contain inaccurate, misleading or downright false information, a negative item can deprive someone of financial credit, auto insurance, bank loans, educational opportunities and many jobs. The latter is especially true in the field of civil service and government employment, which now constitutes almost one-fifth of all the available jobs in the United States.[19]

In other words, people's lives are often severely damaged, even ruined, by today's dossier dictatorship. And one of the most important ingredients in dossiers, for millions of men, is their military record. Yet why should this be?

Why should anyone's military record be in a position to influence everything else he or she ever does in life? Why is an honorable discharge for two or three years' military service axiomatic with the right to live a happy and fruitful civilian life for the next fifty or sixty years? What relevance is a brief, youthful tenure in the unusual world of the military to someone's right to succeed as a civilian?

Most American men do not even have a military record, because most of them were never compelled to serve. Those who did serve, or who at least became entangled in some way with the draft, are thus singled out as the sole group subject to extra scrutiny. They are the only ones whose career opportunities are subject to their having satisfied the unique and often whimsical requirements of a military structure that bears no relationship to the environment they will occupy as civilians. A man's failure to satisfy the military is no barometer of his qualifications to succeed as a civilian. Indeed, some men who excel as soldiers fare poorly as civilians.

The staggering inequities flowing from the whole concept of less-than-honorable discharges can only be corrected in one way: all the various classifications of discharge should be eliminated. Only one document, a certificate of discharge, is needed to show proof of service. No gradations are relevant. Any evaluation of how well or poorly someone did as a military person is pertinent only to the military, and belongs only in its records.

But that is for the future. For the present, for those now suffering the many disabilities caused solely by America's participation in Vietnam, the only just solution is amnesty.

VIII

My entire generation was forced with, I think, an impossible choice, which was between either serving in an ill-conceived and ill-defined war or refusing to serve and either going into exile, going to jail, or going underground. Now I submit that that is an impossible choice, and I think that my whole generation will ask its due for having to be submitted to that choice. And amnesty will be a symbol of that.

—James Reston, Jr.[20]

America's leaders certainly did not deliberately set out on a destructive course in Vietnam. They began with the best of motives, given America's disposition to suspend reason whenever the bugaboo of the Red Menace was raised. But our involvement just grew. No one seemed to know why. No one planned it that way. Soon it was all so huge that it absolutely had to be justified, rationalized, explained.

• We fought to contain China. But when China didn't seem to be going anyplace—

• We fought the North Vietnamese because they were using violence to impose an undemocratic system on another nation. Many other nations around the world were also using violence to impose undemocratic systems on *their* opponents, or indeed upon their own people, and we were not interfering in those struggles. Somehow the blacks of South Africa and the political prisoners in Brazil failed to catch the attention of American leaders bent on freeing people from despotism. Nevertheless—

• We had to subdue the North Vietnamese because they were using inhuman tactics against the South Vietnamese. So we applied even more atrocious methods to defeat them, in the process allowing our standards (which was what the war was all about) to be defined by our enemies. Still—

• We had made treaties and promises to the rulers of South Vietnam. If we withdrew, the world would say we did not honor our treaties. Did our continuation of the war thereby dazzle the court of world opinion? Not, apparently, in such alien cultures as Canada, whose Parliament unanimously condemned our bombing; or Australia, whose Prime Minister gently hinted we ought to stop; or Sweden, whose leaders outspokenly expressed their horror in very public statements; or even our best friend England, whose banner headlines chronicled our dropping of six million tons of explosives on the four tiny countries caught in the war, or three times the total tonnage used in all of World War II. Even so—

• We kept it up, because three consecutive Presidents were not about to be the first to lose a war. They did not seem impressed with the example of one of history's leading warrior-statesmen, General Charles De Gaulle. The General did not concern himself with the semantics of who "won" or "lost" when he sensibly pulled France out of Algeria. He also granted amnesty to most Frenchmen who had resisted the war. These acts not only did not diminish, rather they increased, De Gaulle's stature in world opinion. But although American public opinion against remaining in Vietnam reached as high as 73 per cent in some polls—

• Our leaders would not stop. They would not heed voices such as that of our former Ambassador to Moscow, George F. Kennan, who told the Senate Foreign Relations Committee "there is more respect to be won in the opinion of this world by a resolute and courageous liquidation of unsound positions than by the most stubborn pursuit of extravagant or unpromising objectives."

And what were we saving for democracy? A government so antidemocratic that one of the chief concerns of thoughtful outsiders, as American troop levels decreased, was fear for the lives, health and safety of at least 100,000 political prisoners being held by the Saigon government.[22]

It was a government whose tiger cages, rigged elections and government-controlled press made for rather awkward advertising.

It was a government whose police, even with the signing of the cease-fire treaty in Paris only four days away, could break into a middle-class Saigon home at 3 a.m., ransack the belongings of Nguyen Thi Phuong Tho, and arrest her because they found, in a stack of her books, the lyrics to songs extolling peace. Although no public charges were ever filed against her, Nguyen spent five months in jail, where she said she was beaten until she vomited blood. At the time of her arrest, Nguyen was fourteen years old.[23]

Too many Americans knew what kind of a government we were propping up in Saigon for the war to remain disguised as a crusade for democracy. The combination of an unprecedented war, along with unprecedented conduct by our own government, induced an unprecedented response by the American people. Cries of anguish and anger rose across the land. Members of Congress, state and local officials, priests, rabbis, ministers, prominent businessmen, housewives, doctors, former generals, teachers—all of whom might be expected to have an influence on the young—spoke out publicly against the war. In the eyes of a substantial proportion of the population, it was of the highest priority to stop our leaders from inflicting further suffering, merely to justify a political mistake. To protest was the highest form of patriotism. To reject this war was not to reject America, but to honor it.

Those young men who resisted the military were behaving no differently from millions of others in the population at large. Indeed, as the ones who took by far the greatest risks, and whose idealism awakened many of their elders, they perhaps contributed more than anyone to ending an American disgrace. Before continued punishment for them can be justified, the war they risked so much to stop must be justified first.

IX

> Though I shall always think it a sacred duty to exercise with firmness and energy the constitutional powers with which I am vested, it appears to me no less consistent with the public good than it is with my personal feelings to mingle in the operations of Government every degree of moderation and tenderness which the national justice, dignity and safety may permit.
>
> —George Washington, 1795

As President Washington's words illustrate, amnesty can be the hallmark of a nation strong enough to be magnanimous, and of a leader self-assured enough to be generous. Not only did Washington wipe clean the slate for those Pennsylvania farmers who participated in an actual insurrection—the Whiskey Rebellion—but no effort was made to punish the thousands of men who deserted his army during the Revolution. During the Civil War, Lincoln in effect used amnesty as a weapon, designed to lure Confederates to desert. But he also amnestied men actually guilty of treason. And at war's end, as the Cabinet discussed the question of bringing captured Confederate leaders to trial, Lincoln said "I hope there will be no persecutions, no bloody work after the war is over. No one need expect me to take part in hanging or killing those men, even the worst of them . . ."

"How gratifying it is to recall," exclaimed historian Henry Steele Commager, in testifying to the U.S. Senate, "that the United States put down the greatest rebellion of the nineteenth century, without imposing on the guilty any formal punishment. There were no mass arrests, no punishment even of those officers of the United States Army and Navy who had taken service in the Confederacy."[24]

No less than thirty-four amnesties have been proclaimed by some thirteen American Presidents. Among them were such early giants as John Adams, Thomas Jefferson and James Madison.

Although Woodrow Wilson did not lift a finger to grant amnesty to those punished for evasion in World War I, pardons were eventually granted by his successors, Warren Harding and Calvin Coolidge. What is most striking, however, is that the number who were actually penalized was small in comparison with the number who might have been. For there were nearly 300,000 draft resisters untouched by the law at the end of World War I.[25] They comprised an even higher figure, proportionately, than the rate during Vietnam, yet little effort was made to prosecute most of them. Thus the government, if not Wilson directly, granted a wide de facto amnesty after a war whose popular support was incomparably greater than Vietnam's.

Resistance during World War II was infinitesimal, but even there President Truman created a President's Amnesty Board. Instead of considering resisters as a class, however, the Board processed them on a case-by-case basis, thus actually becoming a pardoning board. The three-man Board plowed through 15,805 cases, meaning that at best it could not have averaged more than a few minutes' time on each. It pardoned only 1,523, or about 10 per cent.* The process turned out to be so irrational

---

*The Board "compiled data concerning the family history, school and work records, criminal records, and selective service history of each individual. In considering this data, the Board used no specific standards or formulae." From Douglas W. Jones and David L. Raish, "American Deserters and Draft Evaders: Exile, Punishment or Amnesty," *Harvard International Law Journal*, 13, (1972), p. 124.

that it rejected, for example, some 4,300 Jehovah's Witnesses (whose faith would surely classify them as conscientious objectors) on the ground that they were not pacifists because they asserted they *would* fight in one war, God's last war, the battle of Armageddon.

Thus the perils of bureaucratic handling, on a case-by-case basis, of a complex and sensitive matter.

While American history certainly provides more than ample precedent for granting amnesty to those who came into conflict with the national law over some large political purpose of the government, amnesty for those suffering the results of our involvement in Vietnam need hardly rely on such precedents, supportive as they may be. For Vietnam was so far outside the pale of anything this nation has ever done before that its circumstances literally make it a separate case. More urgent than the traditional question of whether we may do something because it has been done before, are the questions of national morality, national reconciliation, national justice and the national interest. In addressing all these questions, amnesty for Vietnam resisters transcends the traditional matter of determining the basic guilt or innocence of someone who has broken the law.

Still, there are those for whom the sheer lawlessness of Vietnam is not in itself enough to engender their support for amnesty. Their reluctance is often rooted in their concern—shared by those urging amnesty—for the integrity of law and justice.

X

Such persons generally oppose amnesty because they believe that those who break the law must pay the penalty. Applying this rule to Vietnam, one must ask how these people would reconcile the thousands of situations like that involving the two sons of a barber in a medium-sized, central California community. As the boys reached draft age, their father worried about their being called. One of his customers was a colonel in the Army Reserves. The barber asked the colonel if there was anything he could do. One week later, the boys were jumped to the very top of the list for their local unit. They were soon Reserves. They never went on active duty, and they never went to Vietnam. They are draft-dodgers.[26]

Should they go to jail? They won't, of course, because they did not break the law. They just "evaded" it. How do these, and hundreds of thousands of other boys like them, differ from those now facing legal sanctions for openly refusing to serve? Mostly, of course, in being white, middle-class, and able to make connections. Those who were drafted were, for the most part, the ones who were already the victims of life's inequities and society's discrimination. They were mostly the poor, the black and the undereducated. It was this circumstance which caused them to break the law directly while others broke it indirectly.

Do those insisting upon "justice" really mean it? Or do they actually mean they approve of one kind of justice for some, and a different kind for others. Do they attach more respect to those who violated the draft laws covertly than to those who resisted them openly? Are they teaching their children, in effect, that the word "justice" means it is all right to bend or break the law so long as you can get away with it? And that those who have the means can therefore avoid the penalties paid by those who haven't? If not, if they deny that these are the standards they are applying, then how can they advocate further discrimination (punishment) against those who are already being punished?

This is not to say that anyone who commits any crime may cite his underprivileged background as an excuse for automatic pardon. If the law is being applied in an essentially even-handed way, to rich and poor, black and white, it is fair enough to insist that violators pay the penalty. But we are talking here about specific laws—the draft laws—and their use during the Vietnam war.

It has always been axiomatic, in appraising our system of justice, that to fulfill its role of maintaining an orderly society, the dispensation of justice must not only *be* fair, it must also have the *appearance* of fairness. Without this, justice—no matter how high-principled—could not hold the general respect upon which it depends for its effectiveness.

It has also been axiomatic, in appraising our system of conscripting men for the Vietnam war, that any resemblance between the operation of the draft, and the definition of the word fairness, was not only incidental, it was all but invisible. The draft was so utterly unfair, so totally lacking in consistency, so inefficiently managed and so permeated with compromise, favoritism, exceptions and special privilege that it elicited either the contempt or at best the disrespect of most who came in contact with it. What better measure of the contempt for law which the draft inspired, than the single-mindedness with which the white middle class—the very group always invoked as the backbone of our society—evaded it? Who can now call for justice in the name of a law which epitomized the perversion of justice? How many are there like the successful manufacturer from the Midwest who, having applied his influence to shield his two sons from the draft, proceeded to impugn the patriotism of war protesters and draft-dodgers at every cocktail party and business meeting he attended once his youngest son had passed draft age? It would be hard to find an American who cannot cite examples of "legal" draft evasion from his or her own personal knowledge.

Many people say, in all sincerity and with no spirit of malice, that it would set a bad example for the law simply to ignore the crimes of a large group of people. Social order, they fear, would come unglued.

First of all, this ignores the overriding fact that amnesty is itself a part of the law, dating all the way back to the time of America's founding. Amnesty is mentioned twice in the Constitution, and is part of our statutes and case law.

Beyond this, in view of the fact that an even larger group has already been excused through its ability to evade the law before the fact, rather than after, would it really be serving the law well for it to be used now as an instrument of further discrimination? Might not the law, which has often gained as much stature through its ability to be merciful as well as to be harsh, benefit far more in this instance by applying the former quality rather than the latter? In what way will the influence of justice be strengthened by singling out a relative few—who are already suffering the punishment of homelessness, imprison-ment or exile—while everyone else has already gone free?

Nor does amnesty mean the nation will be unable to raise troops for future wars. Our long history of past amnesties cer-tainly posed no difficulties for conscription in wars preceding Vietnam. This would indicate that it is the particular war, not the consideration of amnesty, that causes resistance. To say otherwise is to say that America can only maintain an army based on fear, and that her sons care so little that even if the issue is freedom and equality, they won't fight. Since all the evi-dence shows that Americans respond handsomely when they believe in a cause, the answer would seem to be to have better wars, not to deny amnesty. There is no historical evidence that amnesty has ever inspired others to disobey the law, or to refuse service in a later war. This is partly because amnesty is *discre-tionary*. No one has any guarantee that because amnesty is granted after one war, it will be granted after another.

As for the belief that amnesty will encourage people to break other kinds of laws, the very enormity of the effort now being required to bring about amnesty, even after an extraor-dinarily unpopular war, would be more than enough to elimi-nate that expectation from the thinking of any potential law-breaker. Besides, amnesty applies to political crimes of a whole class of people, not to individual acts.

Two more points are relevant to the legitimate concern of those who feel that granting amnesty will weaken the rule of law. One is that the law never has, and does not now, come even close to indicting, much less punishing, every violator. This was intended by its framers, as can be seen by the tremendous dis-cretion given to prosecutors. No one can require a prosecutor to prosecute. This gives a democratic society the breathing space, and the law the flexibility, to allow for the civil dis-obedience through which many of America's best instincts, and greatest reformers, have been able to express themselves—to the lasting benefit of us all. As Harrop Freeman has noted:

> We need to recruit these critics of society into the political
> process of changing society, which most everyone recog-
> nizes needs changing. The nation has a profound interest
> in allowing to reformists the most radical means of shak-
> ing us from our lethargy.[27]

The power of discretion also enables prosecutors to reflect
the constant changes in what society deems offensive, and therefore punishable. Who among us, for example, of those who were
adults in the 1930s, would be free of a criminal record today if
the prohibition laws had been strictly enforced? Or to look
ahead, how many of the next generation will the law choose to
prosecute for smoking a marijuana cigarette? Thousands of
laws now on the books are never enforced, sometimes because
they are outdated, sometimes because their violation obviously
poses no threat or danger to society. The failure to enforce 100
per cent of our laws has obviously not undermined our structure as a nation of law.

The final consideration in weighing the possible impact of
amnesty on the rule of law is the question of what is best for
society. Despite the obvious discrimination and unfairness of
the draft that led to the plight of those for whom amnesty is the
only remaining avenue of justice, there are still people who
would single out these young men for punishment. Even the
President of the United States, Richard Nixon, has called for
them to "pay the penalty." The fact is, of course, that many of
them will not be prosecuted, in any case, whether or not amnesty
is ever proclaimed. They will be relieved of formal punishment
because of bureaucratic ineptness, or because prosecutors
choose not to prosecute because the case is too old, or their
caseload is too heavy, or they have other more pressing cases,
or they see the case may not be winnable—or simply because
the general pressure to bring such cases will fade with the passage of time. This narrows even further the small percentage of
those who will be left as the only ones officially selected to "pay
the penalty" for the Vietnam war. Such an act can only be
described as vindictive—and neither great nor wise nations
adopt important policies out of vindictiveness.

Equally important, from the viewpoint of the law's viability, it is impossible to see any benefits that such a vengeful act will bring to society. For it is the good of society that should always be of paramount concern in exercising the law's discretion. What social good will result from imprisoning these young men, and disabling them as felons for the rest of their lives? Prisons, theoretically, are meant to "reform" or "rehabilitate" those who are sent there. Will imprisonment "reform" young men who are being punished for their belief in an idea now shared by most of the nation? Will it teach them not to repeat their crime? How can it cause them not to resist the Vietnam war again, when the war is over for America? Will prison rehabilitate them? They are certainly no threat to anyone's safety, but then, they never were. Indeed, they are in trouble not because they harmed anyone but because they *refused* to.

If anything, by further punishing these young men, society is likely to suffer in ways outside the obvious loss of leadership potential inherent in persons who would risk their entire future for an act of conscience. Imprisonment, and the latter handicap of a prison record, will surely steer some to real crime as a means of survival, once the scarlet letter of a prison record blocks them from meaningful jobs.

XI

Some concerned politicians, in an effort to sound reasonable, are proposing a conditional amnesty, rather than a broad, unconditional amnesty. They see this as a way of gaining support from those who oppose any amnesty at all. Compromise, after all, is the essence of politics, so why not compromise on amnesty?

But how do you compromise on amnesty? Can there be a *partial* forgetting? Can an act be consigned to only partial oblivion? Even if this could be done, how would it be decided which actions would be forgotten? Again, the result would be one more round of discrimination. Again, one last group would remain from among all the victims of the war, to be the victims of one last round of discrimination, to be the ultimate victims of all.

Three types of compromises have been most frequently proposed. The first involves prosecuting only deserters, and granting amnesty to everyone else. This ignores the fact that the only difference between resisters and deserters is that deserters had their eyes opened after induction, while resisters were aware before. This in turn reflects the fact that, generally speaking, resisters tend to be white, middleclass and better educated, while deserters are usually from poorer, less-educated, minority groups. The former had more access to information and counseling beforehand, while the latter were those who simply received a draft notice, went in, and *then* had their eyes opened. There is nothing especially contradictory, indeed, about a young man developing a horror of what we were doing in Vietnam by seeing it for himself, rather than by learning it intellectually. Moreover, there are many examples of deserters who served bravely for extended periods and then, sickened by the pointless killing, and seeing the futility, decided to end their involvement. To distinguish between resisters and deserters would be the most invidious possible form of discrimination.

A second compromise would call for judging each individual separately in a case-by-case hearing. Aside from the fact that this would be monumentally impossible from an administrative point of view, and would take years to complete, it could not be done with any degree of fairness. It would be a mirror of the unevenness and inconsistency of the draft system which entangled these young men to begin with. It would also impose an examination of conscience that would demand an explanation of one's feelings at the time of a decision made as many as eight or ten years earlier. It would amount to an inquisition most theologians would be hard put to pass. It would again discriminate against the least articulate, although their motives may have been the purest of all. And it would be, in any case, an act of cruel presumptuousness for the bureaucracy, with its sterile norms, its hidebound forms, and its narrow frame of reference, to lay its dead hand once more on young men's lives to probe, of all things, the human conscience.

God alone knows what finally determines the actions of
men, and all of us know that few of us do anything for
one reason alone. Therefore we feel it unwise to attempt
to judge the motives of those to be given amnesty, just
as we do not presume to judge the motives of those who
served in the military.[28]

The third compromise would require men to serve two or
three years of alternative service as a form of penitence. This
would not be amnesty at all, of course, since it would be requir-
ing its "beneficiaries" to admit they had done wrong when they
believe they did right.

(The double-edged nature of the claim of "who is right"
was illustrated by a letter from a Vietnam veteran in the Novem-
ber 6, 1972 *Richmond* (Va.) *Times-Dispatch:* "It is not the
deserters and draft-dodgers who failed the country," he wrote,
"but those who failed to question what we were doing.")

Furthermore, the idea of alternative service is based on the
assumption that everyone owes his country two years of his life.
If this is to be the standard, then what of those 88.9 per cent of
all draft-age young men who were never summoned by the draft
in the first place? They never gave two years, were never ordered
to, and are not being asked to now. If everyone really owes his
country two years, then why not everyone? If alternative service
is really to be the means for achieving equitable justice, should
not every American, male and female, draft-involved or not,
serve two years of forced labor? Until that time comes, alternative service would seem a strange way to promote "justice."

XII

Even though amnesty will not diminish the role of law in
our society, it raises other questions. Many of them are perhaps
even more important than issues of legality or history, because
they reach the very deepest emotions of the human spirit.

One of the most compelling of these questions is whether
amnesty is fair to those who served. Didn't those who went to

Vietnam, and sometimes died, replace some of those who refused to go? Not necessarily. The men whose beliefs led them to
refuse to serve had no more to do with another person's being
drafted than the millions who stayed in college to avoid serving,
or who utilized any of the countless other "legal" means of
evasion. (Likewise, those who resisted are no more "cowards"
for their action than those who chose "legal" means of evasion.
Indeed, it could easily be argued that they are far more
courageous.)

Given the fact that the number of men who "legally"
evaded the draft is indisputedly many times larger than the
number who resisted openly, it is clear that no equation could
ever establish that a particular man went because another one
didn't. No one is seeking to punish those millions who evaded
the draft "legally." It would seem less than fair, or logical, to
punish only that small number who acted openly.

Furthermore, had it not been for those who engaged in the
various forms of protest which have resulted in their needing
amnesty, the war would have been much broader, and many
more would have had to bear its burden. By taking the risks
which helped force an end to the war, the resisters made it possible for many others not to go. In the aggregate, they may have
saved many lives.

Still another aspect of this question was raised in an exchange between James Reston, Jr. and former U.S. Attorney
General Ramsey Clark, on the television program, "The Advocates."

> Clark: . . . is it fair to you, as a young man of this
> generation who went to war, that those who refused to
> go not be punished?
> Reston: There has been an attempt throughout
> this amnesty debate to pit one set of victims, those who
> served or those who are casualties or those who died,
> against those who refused to serve. I will not be party to
> that kind of division. I feel we have to attend to all the
> victims of this war, and we will not have this kind of
> division here.[29]

Another problem for some who question amnesty is the feeling that granting amnesty means condoning what the resisters did. Not so. When President Nixon granted executive clemency to James Hoffa, no one interpreted that as presidential approval of jury tampering. Amnesty, likewise, makes no moral judgment. It means, as Ramsey Clark said, "Let's start afresh. Let's start anew. Let's give another chance, another day. Let's look to tomorrow."

Some persons feel that those seeking amnesty should have sought conscientious objector status if they felt so strongly about the war. Many of them did, and were refused. Some of those refusals were arbitrary, others were refused because applicants objected on the basis of war itself, rather than on strictly religious grounds. Ironically, the Supreme Court broadened the test for CO status while the Vietnam war was at its peak, expanding the basis from objection to war on religious grounds to objection to war on moral and ethical grounds.[30] Thus thousands of men who would be classified as COs today must depend upon amnesty instead, essentially for the crime of being a bit ahead of their time.

Many others, mostly the poor and the uneducated, had no knowledge about the provisions of CO status, or had no means of assistance in obtaining it. Thousands of applicants were simply told by their superiors that they were not eligible for CO status, and were harassed for having asked. It was not until 1971 that Selective Service even began publishing information about this legal right. Thousands of men could probably win court cases today, establishing that they were denied CO status either because of false information disseminated by the military, improper actions by the military, or failure of the Selective Service System to advise them of their rights. How much more fitting (and how much more practical) to reach the same end with a proclamation of amnesty instead.

The matter of conscience also addresses the fact that many Americans saw Vietnam as an immoral war, in which the United States was guilty of war crimes. The Nuremberg principles, which the United States supported when many Nazis were being executed for war crimes, state that it is the duty of the individual to resist when ordered to take part in morally reprehensible acts against humanity. Those whose consciences led them to refuse participation in Vietnam because of their belief that we were committing war crimes, were thus obeying a doctrine the United States itself helped establish.

Some will argue, of course, that the Nuremberg principles only apply to persons whose national state is no longer able to defend those who obeyed its orders. To accept this is to say that only those on the losing side must avoid war crimes, while those on the winning side need not, because victors won't be punished anyway. That rationale does not coincide with the principles for which America stands. Indeed, it was presumably our opposition to such a rationale for which we sacrificed so much in Vietnam in the first place.

Other people say amnesty will cause a terrible division within the country. There is as much reason to doubt that expectation as there is to accept it. For one thing, feelings soften with the passage of time. For another, such doomsday prophecies seldom fulfill themselves. Americans are concerned with too many issues to remain critically split over one. It is worthwhile to recall that in the 1960s, the vow of "never" by white Southern segregationists was filled with the same fire and passion some amnesty opponents feel today. But when desegregation came, the world didn't end and the South was not ruined. Instead, it prospered as never before, and the predicted cataclysm never came to pass. Seemingly impossible to accept before it happened, desegregation was not so hard to live with once its irrevocability was firmly established. Likewise the nation may discover that amnesty, once proclaimed, will be a vehicle for reconciliation, not division. As an established part of the law, its acceptance will be aided, too, by the fact that Americans are basically a law-abiding people.

It is also likely that the heat generated by the prospect of amnesty will cool once people in high places, whose stated purpose is to "bring us together," begin tempering their pronouncements with moderation rather than baiting them with meanness.*

This is not to say amnesty will magically be accepted by all the people. That is not its responsibility, anyway. There is a higher responsibility, articulated in the Washington speech by Leslie Dunbar. "We'll not likely find consensus for any position, either for or against amnesty," said Dunbar, but "the search should be for justice, not consensus, and in the long run a just solution may be the best and only path to an enduring consensus."

Perhaps, some say, but in seeking justice, shouldn't those who disobey the law be prepared to pay the price? That question may best be answered with another question: Why? What is so purifying about being punished for seeking justice? True, many have done so, but not because they saw any redemptive quality in absorbing punishment. Rather, there was no other choice: if they were to dramatize the unfairness of a law, they had to do so publicly, which meant being caught and punished. But in the case of politically motivated war resistance, the law does offer a lawful choice—amnesty. Besides, those who resisted have already been punished. Many were brutalized in stockades, such as those at Camp Pendleton who were left hanging from fences for hours in the hot sun. Others have lost years of their lives, unable to start their careers for fear of discovery. Others, who chose exile, are suffering the heartbreak of separation, even ostracism, from their loved ones:

> I will long remember the painful expression, tears rolling down his cheeks, of a 19-year-old Marine war deserter from Jersey City, N. J. who, in a quiet Stockholm bar, shared with me a letter from his father that ended, "You

*President Nixon may not be as opposed to amnesty as his statements indicate. "I can understand how highly motivated individuals could have felt justified in engaging in specific activities that I would have disapproved had they been brought to my attention," he said May 1973. He was describing burglars and political spies then, but hopefully that tolerance will someday extend to young men whose consciences led them to resist war.

have broken our hearts and publicly embarrassed us beyond words. Do not ever come home to this house again."[31]

The subject of parents raises the most tragic question of all: namely, how might those whose sons were killed feel about seeing others receive amnesty? That can only be answered by weighing amnesty in the light of all that has been said here, with four additional thoughts.

First, not all such parents oppose amnesty. Some, in fact, are dedicating themselves to bringing it about. Mr. Robert Ransom, whose son was killed near My Lai a few weeks after the massacre, is a corporate attorney who served four years overseas in World War II. He favors amnesty because

> I can think of no rationale by which the refusal of our government to grant unconditional amnesty would bring me any pleasure whatever, or how it could vindicate the death of my son in any way. My son's life was wasted. It served his country no purpose. That's a fact, and that's behind us.

Mrs. Ransom also favors amnesty, because

> Nothing we can do here or now is going to bring [my son] back, and I guess I can't bear it if we do something that makes it impossible for more sons not to be able to come back home to their families.[32]

Second, the war has already wrought enough suffering. To impose still more suffering on its survivors will not bring back the dead, and certainly such vengefulness will not honor their memory.

Third, the tragedy of losing one's son does not justify denying the return of other sons.

Fourth, the question of why boys were sent to die in Vietnam is properly one addressed to the government of the United States; and the government has not answered it.

Other people object to amnesty because they feel the resisters are claiming to be morally superior. "Of course they're not all moral heroes," says one worker in the amnesty movement. "We should recognize that they are neither heroes nor traitors. Many resisted for many reasons. In a war as insane as Vietnam, why do you have to be a moral hero to do the right thing? That makes no more sense than saying all those who fought in the war did so because they were great patriots."

Which raises a far more troubling question for many who oppose amnesty: If you say the resisters were right, aren't you saying all those who served in Vietnam were wrong? Henry Schwarzschild, Director of the ACLU Foundation's Project on Amnesty, has been asked that question many times. He responds:

> Amnesty makes no judgment about rightness or wrongness. No one who favors amnesty is saying that those who did serve in Vietnam were dishonorable, or that they should not have gone. Most of us do instinctively what the government tells us to do. It is rare for people who are not criminals to disobey the law. It is hard for them.
>
> The war produced neither victory nor honor, but only victims. It victimized all of American society, taking her energy, her resources, her young men's lives. It victimized the young by forcing them to either fight or resist. The GIs, the veterans, the deserters are *all* victims. They are not separate classes.
>
> Society owes these vets a lot. The government should make every redress that can be made, in jobs, education and medical care. And the children of those who died should have every education and health support belonging to their fathers.
>
> Resisters have already paid a price—some, years in stockades or prison. Others, years in exile or living rootlessly, underground, unable to build toward a solid future. Amnesty will not give them back those years, any more than anything can bring back the lives and limbs lost in Vietnam. All have been victimized by the war. Isn't it time to say "enough"?

Time, in other words, for an act of national reconciliation. Time for our young people—an entire generation conditioned by experience to know America only as an institution acting through sheer power and military force—to see that quality of charity, and generosity of spirit, that have made America the great nation she has been and once again can be. Time for a proclamation of universal, unconditional amnesty.

REFERENCES

1. *Burdick* v. *United States*, 237 U.S. 79, 95 (1915). 2. Harrop A. Freeman, "An Historical Justification and Legal Basis for Amnesty Today," *Arizona State University Law Journal* (1971), p. 531. 3. From the Report to the Senate Subcommittee on Refugees and Escapees by the General Accounting Office, May 3, 1972. 4. *Congressional Record*, May 3, 1972, p. S7187. 5. Report to the Senate Subcommittee on Refugees and Escapees by the General Accounting Office. 6. From *When Can I Come Home?*, ed. Murray Polner (New York: Doubleday Anchor, 1972), pp. 49-50. 7. *New York Times*, January 6, 1973. 8. See Frank Donner and Eugene Cerruti, "The Grand Jury Network: How the Nixon Administration Has Secretly Perverted a Traditional Safeguard of Individual Rights," *The Nation*, January 3, 1972, pp. 5-15. 9. Los Angeles Times News Service. 10. Louis Lusky, "Amnesty for Whom, and How Much?", *The National Observer*, March 11, 1972. 11. *Washington Post*, June 9, 1971. 12. Grace Paley, "The Man in the Sky Is a Killer," *New York Times*, March 23, 1972. 13. From a column by D.J.R. Bruckner, *Los Angeles Times*, January 3, 1972. 14. Testimony before the Senate Subcommittee on Administrative Practice and Procedure, Hearings on Amnesty, March 1, 1972. 15. See Leon Friedman and Burt Neuborne, *Unquestioning Obedience to the President: The ACLU Case Against the Legality of the War in Vietnam* (New York: W.W. Norton, 1972). 16. Robert K. Musil, "The Truth About Deserters," *The Nation*, April 16, 1973, pp. 495-499. 17. Douglass L. Curtis, "Due Process and Military Discharges," *Journal of the American Bar Association* 57 (September 1971), p. 875. 18. See Aryeh Neier, "Dissemination of Derogatory Information: A Weapon Against Crime or Part of the Problem?", in *Investigating the FBI*, ed. Pat Watters and Stephen Gillers (New York: Doubleday, 1973), pp. 219-36. Neier is executive director of the ACLU. 19. U.S. Census Bureau figures. 20. A Vietnam veteran himself, Mr. Reston made these remarks on "The Advocates," Public Broadcasting Service, February 22, 1973. 21. From "Amnesty: A Brief Historical Overview," by John C. Etridge, Foreign Affairs Analyst, Library of Congress, February 28, 1972. 22. Report of Amnesty International, London, July 1, 1973. 23. Associated Press dispatch by Dennis Neeld, Saigon, June 24, 1973. 24. Testimony before the Senate Subcommittee on Administrative Practice and Procedure, Hearings on Amnesty, March 1, 1972. 25. U.S. Selective Service System, "Enforcement of the Selective Service Law," Special Monograph No. 14 (1950). 26. Interview with John Hancock, executive director, National Council to Repeal the

Arlie Schardt

Draft. 27. Freeman, "An Historical Justification . . . ", p. 534. 28. Statement of the Interreligious Conference on Amnesty, Washington, D.C., March 27, 1972. 29. "The Advocates," February 22, 1973. 30. *Welsh* v. *United States,* 398 U.S. 333 (1970). 31. Richard Fernandez, executive director of Clergy and Laity Concerned, writing in *American Report,* May 7, 1973 (special issue on amnesty), p. 11. 32. "The Advocates," February 22, 1973.

AMNESTY?
NEVER!

William A. Rusher

Introduction

Amnesty is the formal act whereby a state signifies its decision to refrain from seeking to punish certain persons who have violated its laws. Ordinarily, though not invariably, it is applied to certain broad categories of persons whose crimes involved acts of political protest; and the granting of amnesty thus usually has, and is intended to have, an equally political aspect of "closing the books" on a period of strong controversy. As far as the federal government of the United States is concerned, amnesty has most commonly been proclaimed (if at all) by the President alone, probably by analogy to the undoubted executive prerogative of clemency; but it is clear that amnesty can also be declared by means of a bill duly passed by Congress and signed into law by the President.

It should be noted at the outset that the granting of amnesty is strictly an act of grace on the part of the state. That is to say, the state in no way concedes thereby that its laws are unenforceable, or that they may be violated with impunity. Amnesty, if it is granted at all in a given case, partakes rather of the character of charity, and represents no more than the decision of the state that it will not prosecute a particular offender or category of offenders.

In the history of this country, amnesty has hardly been commonplace, and it has generally been granted only in situations of the type already mentioned, where a mood of political rebellion gripped an entire region, and where amnesty served to cool the embers, once the fire was brought under control. In the specific case of wartime draft-dodgers and deserters, amnesty is simply not a part of the American tradition. On the contrary, *there has never been, in the history of the United States, a general unconditional amnesty for individuals who dodged the draft or deserted in time of war.*

The present position of the United States government, with respect to those who dodged the draft or deserted during the Vietnam war, is entirely in keeping with this record. The policy

57

of the Nixon administration was stated by the President himself at a news conference late in 1972:

> Those who served paid their price. Those who deserted must pay their price, and the price is not a junket in the Peace Corps, or something like that, as some have suggested. The price is a criminal penalty for disobeying the laws of the United States. If they want to return to the United States, they must pay the penalty.

The context indicates that Mr. Nixon did not intend to confine his statement to those who technically "deserted" from the armed forces, as distinguished from those who dodged the draft.

There has been some confusion (which I note Mr. Schardt seems to share) because, in a television interview with CBS newsman Dan Rather on January 2, 1972, Mr. Nixon volunteered that he personally would be inclined to be "very liberal" in the matter of "amnesty." He described "amnesty," however, simply as "the prerogative of the Chief Executive," and it seems clear that what he meant was not that he favored a true and blanket amnesty, but only that he was disposed toward a generous use of executive clemency in the cases of individuals who were convicted of these crimes. This is, of course, in no way inconsistent with his clear determination that they must be punished in some appropriate degree.

The reasons for the reluctance of past and present American administrations to support amnesty for wartime draft-dodgers and deserters are no doubt fairly obvious. Apart from one major and indeed overriding moral consideration (which will be dealt with later under the heading "The Gravity of the Offense"), there are clear reasons of policy. If desertion and draft evasion are allowed to go unpunished, the inevitable result will be to encourage both, in future crises. As former Selective Service Director Curtis Tarr has warned, amnesty would "pave the way toward what in effect would become selective conscientious objection." That is to say, anyone who hereafter disapproves of a particular war would, knowing the precedent for amnesty, feel safe in evading or abandoning military service. And that would be scarcely more tolerable than permitting taxpayers to withhold any portion of their taxes that are to be applied to government expenditures of which they personally disapprove. Such utopian proposals are no doubt fun to contemplate, but they do not have, and in the nature of things cannot have, any cogency in the real world.

The size of the curent problem, in terms of the number of young men who deserted or evaded the draft during the Vietnam war, is difficult to determine. By no means all of them have fled to Canada or Sweden or elsewhere abroad; a great many are "underground" in the United States—living under assumed identities, as fugitives from justice. As of September 1, 1971, 30,259 men administratively classified as deserters from the armed forces were still at large. In the matter of draft evaders, however, reliable statistics are far harder to come by. (The term "draft-dodgers" or "draft evaders," by the way, as used here, includes both those who failed altogether to register for the draft, and those who were called but failed at some point to report for induction. The term does *not* include those who dishonestly alleged some disability and managed to get excused on that account. Such an act is a crime, and should also be prosecuted; but it is obviously a different crime. Nor does the term include—nor ought it to include—individuals who, on the basis of some real disability, or by virtue of an educational deferment or some other status recognized by the law as exempt, managed to avoid being drafted. As with taxes, there is, and ought to be, all the differences in the world between those who lawfully *avoid* the draft and those who illegally *evade* it. Mr. Schardt's effort to equate the two acts strikes at the very heart of law enforcement.)

It is, in any case, safe to say that the number of draft evaders is far higher than the number of deserters. Mr. Schardt, for example, in his section of this book, estimates the combined total at 560,000, although this is surely on the high side.

Equally unclear is the number in both categories who are actually living abroad. An estimated 670 are in Sweden. A much larger number, variously put at anywhere from 7,000 to over 100,000, have found refuge in Canada. These figures are probably not highly important, however, since the various proposals for amnesty, unconditional and otherwise, would apply both to those now abroad and to those "underground" in the United States.

In making his case for conditional amnesty, Senator Hatfield spends considerable time distinguishing various categories of offenders and prescribing what he considers appropriate treatment for each:

1. Total amnesty for draft-dodgers (but apparently not deserters) who elected to stay in this country and go to jail rather than decamp to Canada or Sweden;

2. Amnesty on a case-by-case basis for draft-dodgers (but not deserters) now "underground" or abroad, who voluntarily submit themselves to the decision of specially created "Amnesty Appeal Councils," which would be empowered to "recognize the legitimacy of 'selective' conscientious objector status"—a principle that Senator Hatfield has, however, been notably unsuccessful in persuading any Congress elected by the American people to accept;

3. A rough analogy to amnesty for bona fide conscientious objectors, who are already spared from military service under existing laws but who are presently required to perform, and are performing, some sort of "alternative service," and who Senator Hatfield believes should be spared even this obligation; and finally,

4. Amnesty on a case-by-case basis for deserters, apparently whether they reappear and request it or not, with the decision on punishment (if any) being made by a separate special tribunal charged with distinguishing garden-variety desertions from those that take place in combat situations.

I have no comparable section in this third of the book because, as I demonstrate later ("The Options Available Under the Law"), all of the needful distinctions can and would be made under our normal legal processes of prosecution, conviction, sentencing, and executive clemency, without anybody having to invoke the sweeping principle of "amnesty" at all. Senator Hatfields's intricate distinctions and special quasi-judicial tribunals are reminiscent of G. K. Chesterton, who once remarked that he had labored to construct a theological heterodoxy—only to discover, when he had finished it, that it was orthodoxy.

The Duties of Citizens and the Rights of States

Since advocates of amnesty for Vietnam war resisters are fond of contending, quite inaccurately, that amnesty in comparable cases is "a part of the American tradition," it will be necessary to examine the historical record in some detail. Before doing so, however, and then going on to weigh the case for amnesty for Vietnam war draft-dodgers and deserters, let us consider the duties of citizens and the rights of states from a more philosophical standpoint. By what right does a state presume to draft its young men for military service anyway? And how absolute is the obligation of an individual to obey his country's laws, and specifically its draft laws, if doing so is morally repugnant to him?

On close inspection, these questions prove intricate and troublesome. Across the centuries, a whole series of rather ambiguous formulae testify to the underlying presence of a knotty problem. Jesus, when asked about paying Roman taxes, advised, "Render unto Caesar the things which are Caesar's, and unto God the things that are God's." Chief Justice Coke, challenging the absolutist pretensions of James I, flung down his famous dictum, *"Non sub homine sed sub Deo et lege"* ("Not under man but under God and law")—a piece of wisdom that so impressed Harvard Law School that they inscribed it over the central entrance to Langdell Hall. More recently still, Boston's famed Cardinal O'Connell sought to reconcile his civic and spiritual obligations by insisting, less elegantly but no less adroitly, "I take my religion from Rome and my politics from home."

In its modern and generic form, the central problem can be stated as follows: Is the obligation of a citizen to obey his country's laws technically absolute, or are there circumstances under which he is justified in disobeying a law in obedience to some higher imperative, either extrinsic or intrinsic to himself? And, if disobedience is at times morally justified from the standpoint of the individual, what are the pragmatic and/or moral rights (if any) of the state, in the face of such disobedience?

The answer to these questions will of course depend, in the first instance, upon whether we regard an individual human being as merely a subordinate cell of a larger social organism or, socially speaking, as an autonomous entity. I mention the former possibility not because it has ever claimed any significant support in the Western world but because the concept has an impressive pedigree elsewhere, and may even be the best way of describing the attitude of certain modern states (say, the People's Republic of China) toward their citizens. For the inheritors of the Western tradition, however, there really can be no argument about it: each human being is, in social terms, an autonomous entity, and his relation to the state, whatever else it may be, is the relation of one entity to another.

This quality of "otherness" causes no particular problem so long as the state is perceived by the individual as the source of *moral* authority—i.e., of the very definitions of what is "right" and "wrong" for the individual. Thus, a king who is believed to be a god, or to be ordained by God to rule without limitations, obviously cannot logically be disobeyed on moral grounds. But the slow secularization of the European states, from at least the time of the Reformation forward, gradually and inevitably gave rise to an acute form of the problem I have mentioned. (Coke's dictum was one major step in this process, as it unfolded in England.) For men soon found themselves uncomfortably beholden to two masters: one an increasingly secular state, which made laws and sought to compel its citizens' obedience thereto, and the other a transcendental moral authority (originally almost always identified as God or His Church, but nowadays often described simply as the individual's autonomous "conscience"), whose imperatives were by definition binding and might from time to time conflict irreconcilably with some law enacted by the state.

It was a real dilemma for individuals grounded in the Western tradition, since obviously one master or the other had to be disobeyed. And since, for autonomous Western man at any rate, a transcendental moral imperative is superior to the command of the state, it followed that it is the state that must, in such a crisis, be disobeyed (unless, of course, as happens neither infrequently nor improperly, the individual is unsure of the soundness of his moral intuition and chooses to yield to the state's command in spite of it).

But, if this is the necessary answer to the problem from the standpoint of a given individual, no state can be expected to leave the matter there, for the very best of pragmatic reasons. For while each individual is an autonomous entity, he also inevitably lives among other individuals in a complex web of social relationships, and the state is the mechanism whereby these relationships are governed and various collective actions are decided upon and carried out. Desirable as it might be in theory, therefore, for the state to allow each individual to obey only those laws that he conceives to be in accord with the higher imperatives of his conscience or his God, it plainly will not do, just as a practical proposition.

To be sure, many modern states are pretty sophisticated about this, and often contrive to let a troubled conscience have its way. (The spectacular example of the United States, of course, is the exemption of "conscientious objectors" from the normal obligation of military service.) But such exceptions, like amnesty itself, are invariably mere acts of grace on the part of the state, and never imply a concession that its laws may be disobeyed simply because they conflict with the commands of the individual conscience.

The same applies to the various recent efforts, some of them at least equally sophisticated, to raise "civil disobedience" to the rank of a recognized and accepted political procedure. In the first place, however, note that if a law is broken, not because the individual feels morally obligated to disobey that particular law, but simply in order to make a political point (e.g., to protest the Vietnam war by blocking traffic in front of the White House, or throwing duck's blood on Selective Service records), then we are not really dealing with a troublesome moral compunction against obedience to those particular laws at all. Instead, we are being confronted with a sort of free-form adjunct to the legislative process: an attempt—not always unsuccessful, by the way—to attract the attention of a complacent majority to the deeply felt wishes of an impassioned minority. In such a situation it may be that the majority will elect to make policy concessions to reduce the incidence of further such "civil disobedience," and will even overlook, as a matter of policy or sheer convenience (but always, again, as a matter of grace), any demonstrative violations of law that have already occurred.

Both situations—the exemption of conscientious objectors from military service, and those rare occasions on which "civil disobedience" may be allowed to go unpunished in fact—represent rough parallels to the granting of amnesty. But they share, too, its basis in an act of grace; neither concession implies for a moment that the state's laws may be broken at will.

Indeed, as I have already suggested, the case for a secular state's absolutist position in this matter of obedience seems, from a purely pragmatic standpoint (the only one presently under discussion), unassailable. One simply cannot, for example, have half the population driving on the right, while the other half, or even a stray exception here and there, is determined to obey what it perceives to be a higher moral imperative to drive on the left. The same is true of the tax laws, the draft laws, and indeed all laws—save perhaps those (e.g., the laws against gambling and fornication) which are on the books not so much to be enforced as to codify the official moral opinion on various controversial topics. But while such a pragmatic rationale may serve as adequate justification for the commands of a secular state, it clearly cannot dictate the response of an individual who truly feels unable, on grounds of conscience, to obey a particular law. What course is legitimately open to such a person?

Before answering that question, however, there arises an important collateral point having to do with the legislative procedures of the state that has issued the unacceptable command. Secular states are, of course, not "moral beings" in the sense that individual humans are; they are simply social organisms growing out of social necessities. States therefore cannot be said to have moral motivations, obligations and rights in the same way, or to the same degree, that individuals do. But I do think that a state's way of arriving at its laws can affect, if not an individual's ultimate response to those laws, at least what might be termed the state's "moral right" to punish one of its citizens if he is conscientiously compelled to disobey.

In a totalitarian state, a dissenting individual can have no effective voice in the formulation of the laws. In Communist countries, for example, the laws of the state are based upon the supposed "laws of history" as adduced by Marx and Lenin. In such a system, an individual who happens to disagree with the Marxist interpretation of history has no opportunity even to propose social policies (i.e., laws) based upon other premises. He is, in effect, a political prisoner; and as such he has the right of anyone unjustly imprisoned: namely, to rebel against his jailers in any way he can—although, as we have noted, the state will of course not see matters that way.

In a democracy on the other hand (and I do not think it is necessary to linger over all the complexities that can be factored out of that much-labored term: I am speaking of the ordinary, typical, representative democracy, and what I say is applicable to any of democracy's numerous varieties, *mutatis mutandis*), the situation is significantly different. In any state, and certainly in a nation of over 200 million people such as the United States, the influence any one person can have on the legislative process is quite likely to be very small. But in a democracy the *possibility* of influence is certainly there—indeed, in the case of the United States it is constitutionally guaranteed. In modern American political theory, therefore, and (even more important) in practice as well, no legislative options are theoretically foreclosed, and every individual is guaranteed the right to propose, or oppose, the enactment of any laws he chooses. Whether he succeeds depends in the last analysis only upon how many of his fellow citizens he can persuade to follow his lead. (It is true that before eighteen-year-olds could vote, their influence on legislation directly affecting them, including the draft laws, was limited by their lack of that right. But some age limit on the franchise is inevitable, even though our laws may profoundly affect those without it, and the validity of the laws can therefore hardly be attacked on that ground alone. Should girls of fourteen have more influence on the laws concerning statutory rape? Should children of ten participate in the selection of truant officers? Should we appoint a proxy for foetuses, and let him cast their votes in referendums on abortion?)

This combination of techniques—minority rights and majority rule—profoundly alters, it seems to me, the moral landscape in a democracy. Because while any individual is, as we saw, ultimately answerable only to his conscience in the matter of whether to obey a law, and while any state can be expected, on unassailable pragmatic grounds, to seek to punish all who disobey, a democracy may further be said to have a *moral right* to do so—a right a totalitarian state does not have.

The point does not, I think, require much explication. Each of us no doubt is an autonomous moral entity, answerable in the last analysis only to himself. But so is every one of the rest of us—more than 200 million of us. There is simply no way to avoid frequent collisions between the conflicting individual moral imperatives present in such a population: some must prevail, and others give way. And it is not hard, I think, to perceive, in the democratic provision that the majority's preference shall prevail, the basis for a "moral right" of sorts on the part of the state as representative of the majority of its citizens. If we *must* lead lives that to some degree tread upon each other, and if collective decisions *must* be made (concerning military service, and much else) that will satisfy the moral imperatives of some individuals but inevitably run counter to the moral imperatives of others, then let us make those decisions that offend the moral imperatives of as few as possible—and require that minority to abide by those decisions so far as may be necessary for their effective implementation, until and unless they can recruit enough allies to reverse or modify them.

(I have assumed above that the majority's conscience will not decree the enactment of laws that would effectively destroy the rights of minorities to work for change. If the majority does, however, embark upon such a policy of repression, it of course loses any semblance of a *moral* right to punish those citizens who disobey it.)

But not even the possession, on the part of the state, of a moral right to enforce its laws can alter the individual's paramount obligation to his God and his conscience, and he may be so unfortunate as to find himself in a situation where this squarely conflicts with the state's insistence that he obey. In such a case, so far as I can see, the individual has only one legitimate option: to disobey the offending law and suffer the prescribed penalty for doing so—unless he prefers to leave the state and its jurisdiction altogether.

In this analysis, please note that a democracy does not lose its moral right to punish an individual who violates its laws simply because the individual in question personally considers the society undemocratic and hence morally disqualified to punish him. The individual's perceptions are, no doubt, necessarily determinative of *his own* attitudes and actions; but a general social policy must be discussed from the standpoint of general perceptions.

The point is largely of only technical interest anyway, since even a truly totalitarian society might conceivably think of itself as essentially democratic, and hence regard itself as not only pragmatically but morally justified, precisely in terms of the analysis we have made, in punishing those who violate its laws. The argument then becomes circular, with the society conceiving of itself as democratic, and the rebellious individual perceiving it as totalitarian, and both acting accordingly. In this discussion, however, for whatever it may be worth, I take it to be the independent general perception of mankind that the United States today is democratic, in the sense and to a degree which, I have argued, justifies it, not only pragmatically *but morally,* in punishing those who violate its laws.

Young people today who profess to disagree with this view (of the United States as a democracy) often betray a genuine confusion as to precisely what a "democracy" is, and come dangerously close to defining it as a society in which they have their way. As an American conservative, I feel almost uniquely qualified to disabuse them on that score. I personally have had a lively interest in American politics for thirty-seven years, and have played a fairly active role in them for a quarter of a century. Yet the number of times I have been on the winning side is poignantly small. This does not prove, however, that America is undemocratic—merely that my causes, candidates and preferences have usually been those of a minority.

The History of Amnesty in America

Having analyzed in philosophical terms the limits of an individual's duty to obey the state's laws, and the state's rights in the event of such disobedience, let us now look at the historical record, to discover what this country's official attitude toward amnesty, and especially amnesty for draft-dodgers and deserters, traditionally has been.*

---

*In this section I have rearranged, condensed and sometimes paraphrased, but carefully followed, the scholarly study by John C. Etridge of the Congressional Research Service, to whom I acknowledge my profound indebtedness.

As already noted—and as might be expected, in view of what has been said concerning the quasi-political nature of most acts of amnesty—those which have occurred in the history of the United States have usually been addressed not to instances of draft evasion or desertion but to episodes of open rebellion against the authority of the United States government.

The very first example of an amnesty in United States history was of this type. In the Whiskey Insurrection of 1794, "several hundred men," protesting an excise tax on whiskey, burned the home of the regional inspector of the excise for western Pennsylvania and tarred and feathered a number of federal revenue officers, President Washington ordered the insurgents to return to their homes, called for militia for Pennsylvania and three nearby states, and directed that the rebellion be put down by force. The western counties of Pennsylvania were thereupon occupied, and more than a score of prisoners were sent to Philadelphia for trial.

On July 10, 1795, however, when the insurrection was long over, Washington proclaimed "A full, free and entire pardon to all persons . . . of all treasons . . . and other indictable offenses against the United States committed within the fourth survey of Pennsylvania before the said 22nd day of August last past . . . " Exceptions were made (significantly) of those who "refuse or neglected to give assurance of submission to laws of the United States."

Other examples of this kind of amnesty are reasonably common. In 1799, over a hundred Pennsylvanians, rebelling this time against the valuation laws for lands and dwellings, freed a United States marshal's prisoners and obstructed him in the performance of his duties. On May 21, 1800, President Adams granted "a full, free, and absolute pardon to all and every person or persons concerned in said insurrection . . . of all treasons, misprisions of treason, felonies, misdemeanors, and other crimes by them respectively done or committed against the United States . . ."

During the War of 1812, President Madison proclaimed an amnesty for the pirates and smugglers around New Orleans who had nevertheless had the good taste to help the forces of the United States in their battle against the British.

The Civil War was, of course, by far the most productive episode in American history in the matter of rebellions against the authority of the United States, and hence in the matter of subsequent amnesties as well. Here, however, it must be remembered, we are dealing with the secession of eleven states of the Union, many or most of whose citizens had been taught to regard those states as individually sovereign. It can have been no easy matter for such people to determine where their civic obligation lay, even assuming they were perfectly willing to perform it if only they could identify it.

Ultimately, of course, the outcome of the war settled that question. As early as 1862, however, the processes of amnesty were at work in certain selected cases where this was deemed appropriate. On February 14 of that year, acting through Secretary of War Stanton, President Lincoln directed the release of many political prisoners and others held in military custody "on their subscribing to a parole engaging them to render no aid or comfort to the enemies in hostility to the United States."

In the Confiscation Law of 1862 (12 Stat. 592), Congress authorized the President to extend pardon and amnesty to persons participating in the rebellion, with such exceptions and upon such conditions as he deemed expedient. Lincoln invoked this statute in subsequent proclamations, without conceding its implicit suggestion that it was his only authority.

On December 8, 1863, President Lincoln proclaimed that

> Whereas it is now desired by some persons heretofore engaged in said rebellion to resume their allegiance to the United States and to reinaugurate loyal State governments . . . a full pardon is hereby granted to them and each of them, with restoration of all rights of property, except as to slaves and in property cases where rights of third parties shall have intervened . . .

Each person pardoned was required to subscribe to and

"maintain . . . inviolate" a prescribed oath of loyalty to the United States. Certain classes of rebels were excepted.

This amnesty must have proved popular with a good many dubious types, for on March 26, 1864, President Lincoln issued a further proclamation stating that the previous proclamation had not been intended to cover civil and military prisoners, but only persons at large who took the oath "with the purpose of restoring peace and establishing the national authority."

Shortly after succeeding to the presidency in the closing days of the Civil War, Andrew Johnson on May 29, 1865, issued a Proclamation of Amnesty and Reconstruction which granted a full pardon to all former Confederates (except certain leaders) who took an unqualified oath of allegiance to the United States. Congress, now in the hands of those who wanted Draconian measures against the South, took sharp exception to Johnson's gentler policy, and early in 1867 repealed the amnesty section of the Confiscation Act of 1862 under which it believed the President was acting. Johnson, however, took the by now traditional presidential view that he could proclaim an amnesty all by himself, and proceeded to do exactly that in three successive proclamations in 1867 and 1868—pardoning all participants in the late rebellion, at first with certain exceptions, and finally with no exceptions whatever.

Congress was outraged, but took no effective action. But with the ratification of the Fourteenth Amendment in July 1868 Congress was given broad new authority in this field; for Section 3 of the amendment barred from state or federal office any person who, having previously taken an oath as a state or federal officer to support the Constitution, engaged in the rebellion— and then provided that this disability could be removed by a two-thirds vote of both Houses. Congress spent ten happy years removing the disability from various individuals, then turned to conferring limited amnesties applicable to all. Finally, in 1898 —a third of a century after the end of the Civil War, when almost all of the leading Confederates were dead anyway—a universal amnesty bill was passed at last.

The next instance of amnesty in American history occurred just four years later, on July 4, 1902, when President Theodore Roosevelt proclaimed a "complete pardon and amnesty" for those who had participated in the Philippine Insurrection. (This, of course, was the insurrection in favor of Philippine independence, led by Emilio Aguinaldo. It began in 1898, and was ended by U.S. military action in 1902.)

In 1917, in an effort to cushion the impact of a Supreme Court decision that threatened to compel enforcement of several thousand federal criminal sentences which had long been supposed permanently suspended, President Wilson amnestied certain categories of persons who would otherwise have been affected by the decision.

The above are—*with the exception* of the relatively few cases involving those who evaded the draft or deserted the armed forces, which will be discussed below—the only instances of amnesty in American history. And I think it is fair to say that, in their general outline, they follow the pattern I described in my introduction: they were acts of grace designed (in most cases) to assist in cooling the embers of dead controversies. Even so, it is striking how cautious America's Presidents and Congresses have been about granting amnesty until the controversy in question was well and truly over, and until those amnestied were clearly willing to submit to the authority of the United States.

Now, what about the special case of amnesties for draft-dodgers and deserters? There are a few such instances in American history, and they constitute the *only* direct analogy to the plea now being made for a general amnesty for Vietnam war resisters. Do they strengthen that plea?

The first amnesty of this type in the history of the United States was proclaimed by President Jefferson on October 15, 1807. It offered a full pardon to all deserters from the Army of the United States who surrendered themselves within four months. *Note that America was at peace at the time of the desertions.*

President Madison was apparently following this precedent when he issued three similar proclamations in February and October 1812 and June 1814—the last two during the hostilties with Britain which are now known as the War of 1812. No exceptions or conditions were specified, but it seems logical to assume that those deserters who surrendered were required to complete their military service, rather than simply drift away—especially during wartime.

In 1830 President Jackson, following Congress's repeal of the death penalty for *peacetime* deserters, pardoned such deserters—subject, however, to the provision that those in prison were to be returned to duty.

The Civil War was the first occasion since the War of 1812 in which amnesty was extended to wartime deserters, and the striking point here is how sparingly, and how conditionally, it was granted. On March 10, 1863 President Lincoln proclaimed amnesty for deserters who reported to the authorities on or before April 1. These were *returned to their regiments,* and of course forfeited all pay and allowances for the period of their absence.

In February 1864 the War Department directed that sentences of death against deserters be *reduced to imprisonment,* and authorized generals to return them to duty whenever this was deemed beneficial to the service.

Under an act of Congress approved March 3, 1865, as the war was drawing to a close, forfeiture of citizenship was specified as the punishment for desertion, but the President was directed to offer a pardon to all deserters who *returned to their posts* within sixty days, and served a period of time equal to the term of their original enlistment. Lincoln did so, in a proclamation dated March 11.

On July 3, 1866, more than a year after the war had ended, the War Department offered amnesty, apparently on similar terms, to all regular army deserters who surrendered before August 15.

No general amnesty of any type was ever proclaimed for

those who deserted or dodged the draft in World War I, despite the fact that under a law enacted on August 22, 1912, deserters forfeited their citizenship. In 1924 President Coolidge did grant amnesty to (and thus restored the citizenship of) some one hundred individuals, who had *deserted after the Armistice.*

In 1933 President Roosevelt granted amnesty (and citizenship) to World War I draft-dodgers *who had completed their sentences.* This carefully limited and highly technical action was the only act of grace ever proclaimed by the U.S. government in respect of those who violated its draft or desertion laws during World War I.

The draft-dodgers and deserters of World War II were scarcely more fortunate. On December 23, 1946, nearly a year and a half after V-J Day, President Truman created an Amnesty Board to investigate individually the cases of 15,805 persons who had evaded or otherwise violated the Selective Service Act during World War II. Exactly a year later, on December 23, 1947, acting on the recommendations of this board, President Truman individually pardoned 1,523 of these men—or *less than 10 per cent.* Deserters, it appears, were *not pardoned at all.*

On December 24, 1952, President Truman issued a proclamation restoring the civil rights of persons who had deserted between July 14, 1945 and June 25, 1950 (in effect, *between* the end of World War II and the outbreak of the Korean war) *and* who had been court-martialed or dishonorably discharged therefor.

No amnesty of any type has been proclaimed by any President of the United States for those who dodged the draft or deserted since the start of the Korean war, nearly a quarter of a century ago.

What, then, of the breezy contention that amnesty for men who have deserted the armed forces or evaded the draft is "as American as apple pie"? On the contrary—it bears repeating—*there is not a single instance of a general unconditional amnesty for wartime draft-dodgers or deserters in the entire history of the United States.*

*The Arguments for and Against Amnesty for Vietnam
Draft-dodgers and Deserters*

We are now in a position to consider on its merits the case
for conferring amnesty on the Vietnam war draft-dodgers and
deserters. Do they fall within the category of conscientious objectors, who are specifically exempted from military service? If
not, is there a *new* principle of international law (derived from
the judgments against the Nazi offenders at Nuremberg) which
justifies their disobedience of American law, and hence would
justify amnesty? Or simply taken all in all, was their disobedience of a sort that can be said to deserve amnesty as a matter of
grace, now that America's military participation in the Vietnam
war is substantially ended?

CONSCIENTIOUS OBJECTION. I have already touched on
the subject of "conscientious objectors," noting that certain
sophisticated modern states, including the United States, have
long made it a policy, simply as an exercise of grace, to excuse
from the obligation of military service individuals whose moral
conscience was profoundly offended by such an activity. The
American statute applies to individuals who have religious
scruples against participating in *any* war. This has recently
been extended by the Supreme Court to include *any* conscientious moral objection, whether grounded in a religious belief
or not; but the requirement is carefully preserved that the objection must be convincingly demonstrated to be against service in *any* war, and not just against service in a particular war
of which the individual happens to disapprove.

Such "conscientious objectors" are, fortunately, easily dis-
tinguishable from those who refused to serve in, or who deserted
from, the U.S. armed forces because of their specific objection
to the American military action in Vietnam. In most cases, the
latter—to their credit—did not and do not pretend to object to
all wars. We are perfectly free to assume that, in a war more to
their liking, they would be quite capable of killing their fellow
men in accordance with the rules, such as they are, of warfare.

They are not, then, "conscientious objectors" at all, in a sense that would bring them within the scope of our present laws on the subject.

THE NUREMBERG PRINCIPLE. But if the Vietnam draft-dodgers and deserters have waived any claim to the status of true conscientious objectors, many of them have been quick to invoke the principle supposedly laid down at Nuremberg, in the postwar trial of the surviving Nazi leaders.

The Nuremberg judgments were based on the principle, which was new to international law (and which is certainly subject to criticism, though in what follows we shall assume its validity), that an agent of a sovereign state may be held personally responsible for "crimes against humanity" which he commits in his capacity as such agent and in response to the orders of the state, speaking through his superiors. (Previously an agent had been spared punishment, even for brutal acts, if they were committed on the orders of his superiors.) The Vietnam deserters and draft-dodgers argue that various deliberate acts of the U.S. armed forces in Vietnam (e.g., bombing villages believed hostile, etc.) constituted precisely such "crimes against humanity"; that they would have been transgressing the Nuremberg principle if they had participated in those acts; and that accordingly they should not be prosecuted for refusing to serve in the U.S. armed forces.

The chief problem with this argument (aside from the invalidity of the principle as a matter of logic and law—which is waived here) resides in the central weakness that the Nuremberg principle can only, as a practical matter, be invoked effectively against the agents of a state which has been defeated in war, or is for some other reason unable to defend those who obeyed its orders. Certainly no still-existing state can reasonably be expected to excuse disobedience of its commands on the ground that to have obeyed them would have constituted a "crime against humanity." To be sure, this may very possibly compel a soldier confronted with an unpalatable battlefield order to base his response on a guess as to which side will win the war. But no one can very well hope to escape uncertainties that are rooted not in logic but simply in the survival prospects of the state to which one owes allegiance.

No doubt some of those who favor amnesty for Vietnam draft-dodgers and deserters would like to bring about (or would even argue that there has already occurred), within the still-existing American society, a revulsion against United States actions in Indochina so profound as to constitute a retrospective judgment that those actions were indeed "crimes against humanity," and that consequently citizens who broke the law by refusing to participate in them are, on the Nuremberg principle, excellent candidates for a collective act of grace. But, however convincing such a line of reasoning may be to many of those who passionately opposed the Vietnam war, it is manifestly not true that the American society *as a whole* has reached any such drastic conclusion about this country's actions in Indochina. And that being the case, any serious arguments based on application of the Nuremberg principle simply collapses.

THE "WRONGNESS" OF THE VIETNAM WAR. Most advocates of amnesty seem to recognize this when they put forward a rather different argument, which constitutes perhaps the commonest and most popular way of stating the case. It seeks amnesty for these young men not as a matter of legal right but as the traditional act of grace, based on compassion.

Let us concede (so this argument goes) that America's actions in Vietnam were not "crimes against humanity." They were, however, unquestionably the subject of wide and profound disagreement within the country, almost from the outset. And, if we can believe the public opinion polls, there is considerable evidence that a majority of the American people came ultimately to believe that at least our national involvement in a ground war in Indochina was somehow "wrong." Certainly the Nixon administration pursued a conscious policy of "winding down" that involvement—a policy very different from that of the Kennedy and Johnson administrations. That being the case, individuals whose only crime was to refuse to participate in that discredited war should, it is argued, be spared punishment by an act of amnesty. (This general line of argumentation can be decorated with any desired amount of rhetorical parsley. Thus, it is sometimes said that the "only real crime" of the draft-dodgers and deserters was to be "prematurely right" about the Vietnam war.)

Let us consider this argument in some detail. In the first place, note the basic proposition: that since this governmental policy, fully supported by appropriate laws, was (allegedly) subsequently reversed, those who violated the implementing laws while they were in effect *therefore* deserve amnesty for their crimes. It is a superficially beguiling idea, but a moment's reflection will reveal the fallacy. Virtually every law is likely to be repealed, or at least fall into desuetude, sooner or later. Citizens must not be encouraged to play guessing games with the state—betting that a given policy will be reversed, violating its legal supports in that cheerful faith, and then living abroad, or incognito, until the reversal occurs, only to emerge triumphant and unpunishable when amnesty is proclaimed. No society could survive for a month if everyone who correctly predicted the subsequent reversal of specific governmental policies went unpunished for violating the laws that implemented them. (And that does not take into account the numerous crimes that would undoubtedly be committed by people who, as matters turned out, miscalculated the likelihood that their acts would soon be decriminalized.)

But of course the Vietnam war draft-dodgers and deserters would not qualify for amnesty even if it were to be extended to everyone who violates the implementing laws of a war policy later reversed. For President Nixon's policy in Vietnam was indeed different from that of Kennedy and Johnson, but it fell far short of constituting a flat "reversal" or repudiation of the previous policy. American ground participation in the Vietnam war was decided upon by Kennedy, and hugely augmented by

Johnson, at a time when the South Vietnamese were far weaker than they are today; and Nixon's reduction of U.S. ground force levels, far from simply reversing that policy, required four full years for its completion—four years during which South Vietnam's ability to defend itself was slowly increased to its present point. There has, in other words, never been a clear-cut "reversal" of U.S. policy in Vietnam at all. On the contrary, U.S. ground participation in the Vietnam war was expressly continued by President Nixon (and even expanded, to the extent that U.S. ground forces assisted South Vietnam's pursuit-incursions into Cambodia), and was brought to an end only when the strength of the indigenous ground forces warranted it. During this whole period, draft-dodgers and deserters—far from being vindicated, either by a policy reversal or by events themselves—were, by their continued resistance, simply ratifying their defiance of the evolving policy and laws of the United States.

As a matter of fact, as the above remarks suggest, the whole notion that America's involvement in Vietnam is now almost universally recognized as having been "wrong" collapses upon close inspection. It is a key contention of those who argue for amnesty, and it is almost entirely false.

It is beyond the scope of this book to refight the Vietnam war, but it is vitally important to note that the numerous critics of America's involvement there have been far from unanimous about the *grounds* for their criticism. Opposition to what was happening never, even for a moment, coalesced into agreement on what *ought* to be done. Some observers, to be sure, argued from the outset (and others after long travail concluded) that U.S. participation in any form was a mistake: that the states comprising the former French Indochina should have been left to sink or swim, in the matter of Communist domination. But other authorities certainly did favor, and still favor, economic and military aid to South Vietnam; and still others argued that American military participation was also proper and desirable, provided it was confined to air strikes and logistical support and did not involve the use of American ground forces.

William A. Rusher

Still other analysts of the problem had no fundamental objection even to the use of American ground forces in Indochina, but were bitterly critical of Defense Secretary McNamara's policy of "incremental escalation"—the strategy of increasing the military pressure *gradually,* thus (these critics contended) always leaving the enemy time to brace for the next blow. At the hawkish end of the spectrum of critics were those—and they were never few—who favored full American participation in the war, and regretted only that this country had not (as it most certainly could have) used its full arsenal of weapons to bring North Vietnam to its knees in a matter of days.

Sharp criticism of the Vietnam war could and often did center, therefore, not on the fact of war, but on the way in which the American government waged it. That is why the opinion polls which occasionally reported a negative majority in reply to such questions as "Do you favor President Johnson's conduct of the Vietnam war?" were so meaningless. The fact of criticism was certainly not inconsistent with the view that this country's involvement was at bottom entirely justified, both morally and strategically. Since such a view strikes many superheated opponents of the war as inconceivable, let us take the time to spell it out.

The United States is by far the strongest nation—indeed, the only superpower—in the non-Communist world. As such, many believe, it has an inescapable moral obligation to do what it reasonably can to help other non-Communist countries avoid being swallowed alive by the expansionist imperatives of Communism. (And, despite one or two passages in Senator Hatfield's section of this book which seem to suggest the contrary, no majority of the people of South Vietnam, or of Vietnam as a whole, or for that matter of any other nation anywhere, has ever voluntarily chosen to go Communist.) What the United States can "reasonably" be expected to do will naturally depend upon the nature of the Communist threat (which may be economic, political or military, or some combination of these), and upon broad geographical considerations. Clearly, this country cannot act as the guarantor of every square foot of presently non-Communist territory anywhere in the world. But the Communist drive to conquer Indochina, and perhaps thereafter the entire Southeast Asian peninsula, certainly called for a response of some sort from the United States, in the opinion of many Americans—including, not incidentally, three national administrations. A line had been drawn somewhere, beyond which Communist military aggression would be resisted by military force. And while it can be argued that it would have been better to draw the line at the Thai border, or (as Singapore's Prime Minister Lee Kuan Yew recently suggested, in acknowledged hindsight) west of the Mekong, the decision ultimately made was to hold South Vietnam—and thus far we have not failed.

Indeed, the worst thing "wrong" with the Vietnam war, in the view of many (myself included), was not at all the decision to resist Communist aggression in Indochina, even with American ground forces, but the *way* in which that decision was presented to the American people—in short, neither the military decision nor its implementation, but its political orchestration.

The Democratic Party is understandably sensitive to the favorite Republican charge that "Every Democratic administration in this century has involved America in a foreign war." It is technically true: Wilson took America into World War I; Roosevelt consciously maneuvered it into World War II; Truman was President when North Korea, mistakenly heeding Secretary Acheson's remarks about America's defense perimeters, invaded the South. When Kennedy, and later Johnson, felt impelled to bring American military pressure to bear on the crisis in Vietnam, they must have dreaded the reaffirmation of this powerful debaters' point. It was for this reason, I think, that they chose to *sidle* into the Vietnam involvement, rather than to proclaim the new policy openly. Congress, of course, was well aware of what was happening, and perfectly willing to acquiesce in it; appropriations for the war sailed repeatedly through both Houses, without benefits of a technical declaration of war. The American people themselves were likewise not uninformed, but they were most certainly not properly prepared. The tragic consequence of this lateral shuffle into war was that no concerted attempt was ever made to summon and unite the spirit of the war effort.

No doubt it can be argued that the attempt would have failed; by the early 1960s, when it was called for, there were divisive forces at work in the American society with which previous administrations, waging previous wars, had not had to contend. But the fact remains that the effort was never made; and as the decade dragged on, and our losses in blood and treasure grew steadily greater, the lack of this original and fundamental preparation of the American public for sacrifices began to take a fearful psychological toll.

Congressional assent, crucial to our form of democracy, was never lacking; and even plebiscitary assent, as measured by the public opinion polls, never registered a popular majority clearly against the whole war effort. But the technical omission to declare the war (to mention just one aspect of the problem) had grave consequences. We were treated to the spectacle of well-known American public figures—both former public officials like Ramsey Clark and movie stars like Jane Fonda—touring the enemy capital, viewing with horror alleged American bomb damage, and interviewing selected prisoners of war: acts that deserved to be, and normally would have been, categorized and punished as treasonable. It is hard to describe the political mismanagement of America's entry into the Vietnam conflict, and its consequences, as anything but a catastrophe.

(Inept though America's entry into the Vietnam war may have been, by the way, there is no basis whatever for the claim, sometimes asserted on behalf of draft-dodgers and deserters, that the failure of Congress to declare the war somehow *legally* excuses their crimes. This contention has been tested in the courts, and has consistently been rejected. In the first place, a man's obligation to serve in the armed forces is not, and never has been, contingent upon a declaration of war. In the second, the courts have consistently held that Congress, by consciously and repeatedly appropriating funds to prosecute the war, legitimized it sufficiently for any purpose that would have been served by a formal declaration. As the United States Court of Appeals for the First Circuit held in *Commonwealth of Massachusetts* v. *Laird* (451 F.2d 26 [1971]), "in a situation of prolonged but undeclared hostilities, where the executive continues to act not only in the absence of any conflicting Congressional claim of authority but with steady Congressional support, the Constitution has not been breached." The Supreme Court of the United States denied *certiorari*.)

It is in this general political and military context that one must view the shift of American public opinion, as reflected in the polls, toward a conclusion that the American involvement in the Vietnam war was in some way "wrong." By 1969, almost everybody was dissatisfied with American participation in the Vietnam war for *some* reason; but the reasons for this dissatisfaction, as indicated above, varied tremendously and were often flatly contradictory. There is certainly no slightest reason to suppose that a majority of the American people have ever come to a conclusion on the subject similar to that of the draft-dodgers and deserters. Indeed, if we are to be guided by polls, it is worth noting that American public opinion seems heavily *opposed* to a general unconditional amnesty for them.

There is, then, no sound basis for the contention that amnesty is justified by a *general national belief* that America's participation in the Vietnam war was, in retrospect, "wrong," either morally or strategically.

Despite this, or perhaps because of it, the proponents of amnesty sometimes seem to be saying that amnesty ought to be granted simply because they and their political allies happen to have opposed strongly the laws that the draft-dodgers and deserters violated, and the war that was then under way. (This, by the way, is also plainly at the bottom of what "conservative"— actually, ultralibertarian—sentiment there has been for amnesty.)

Senator Hatfield's section of this book, for example, seems

to me to consist largely of an eloquent description of his reasons for opposing the Vietnam war and an almost equally eloquent description of his reasons for opposing the draft. Mr. Schardt's attack on the Vietnam war is, to say the least, comprehensive: he not only rings the usual charges on the Pentagon papers, the My Lai massacre, the Kent State tragedy and the awfulness of the war in general, but manages to relate these to Watergate, racism, segregation, class distinctions, inflation, McCarthyism and John Wayne.

But I honestly do not think it takes a Ph.D. in logic to see that these obviously heartfelt denunciations miss the central point. To be sure, Mr. Schardt makes a halfhearted pass at contending that a majority of the American people were "doves" on Vietnam all along, but deep down he must know this is not true —and it is, in any case, untrue whether he knows it or not. The Vietnam war was an issue that bitterly divided the American people, but it was certainly no secret. And, by every test that can practically be employed in a large representative democracy like ours, the successive steps taken with regard to the war by Presidents Kennedy, Johnson and Nixon consistently had (certainly as against the policies advocated by the "doves") at least the grudging support of the majority of the American people. The Presidents were elected by the voters and, necessarily, laid down the basic policy. But six successive Congresses, likewise elected by the people, passed or retained the laws, *including the draft laws,* necessary to maintain that policy. And no attack on the constitutionality of those laws, by Mr. Schardt's ACLU or anybody else, ever got to first base in any court in the land. If that record does not constitute a broad and profoundly democratic mandate for the enforcement of those laws, what would? If the traditional procedures for the democratic determination of this country's policies are to be scrapped or ignored, with what shall we replace them?

My two co-authors must know, far better than most Americans, how bitter was the struggle against the laws whose enforcement they now protest—and how spectacularly futile. Senator Hatfield has been active in American public life for nearly a quarter of a century, and has been a member of the United States Senate since almost the beginning of heavy American involvement in the Vietnam struggle. His views on both Vietnam and the draft would appear to have been honorably consistent, but the important point for our present purpose is precisely that he also consistently failed to win over the necessary majority of his colleagues in the House and Senate to his viewpoint on either subject.

Mr. Schardt has been a prolific writer on behalf of liberal causes, an eyewitness of many of the central events of the 1960s in Washington and elsewhere, and most recently the full-time associate director of the office maintained in Washington by the American Civil Liberties Union for the precise purpose of lobbying in favor of amnesty and related causes.

If Senator Hatfield and Mr. Schardt opposed the draft, they had far better means than most of us to work for its repeal. Why, then, wasn't it repealed before the war ended? Because the Congress—the voice of the American people—refused to repeal it; that's why.

Similarly, the Congress knew perfectly well that America under Lyndon Johnson was becoming steadily more involved in the Vietnam struggle; yet throughout the Johnson administration (and throughout the first Nixon administration as well, despite a Democratic majority in both houses) the war appropriations and other supporting legislation rolled forward in spite of all that Senator Hatfield, Mr. Schardt and their fellow "doves" could do.

If America is indeed a democracy, and the will of the majority as expressed by the Congress and the other institutions of government prevails, it is hard to see why individuals who violate its duly enacted laws should be spared their ordinary punishment at the behest of politicians and lobbyists who unsuccessfully opposed the enactment of those laws in the first place, or unsuccessfully sought their repeal.

DRAFT DODGING AND DESERTING AS "CIVIL DISOBEDIENCE." There is, however, an argument that sidesteps altogether the question whether the Vietnam war was "right" or "wrong." In this version the draft-dodgers and deserters are seen as essentially engaged in a form of "civil disobedience"— i.e., as violating the laws concerning military service not because (or at least not *so much* because) they opposed military service per se, but in order to dramatize to a sluggish and unresponsive majority their personal political opposition to the Vietnam war. The war now being over, and their opposition to it having meanwhile been dignified by what must be recognized as fairly substantial accretions of support, they now deserve to be spared punishment—not precisely in the spirit of a postwar amnesty, but rather by analogy to various alleged recent instances of "civil disobedience" which were, as a matter of policy and grace, not prosecuted to the full extent of the law.

In response, it is fair to ask to what extent "civil disobedience" has in fact contrived to go unpunished in the United States. Almost all of its best-known practitioners, including the late Martin Luther King, Jr., have been sentenced to varying terms in jail for criminal acts committed for purposes essentially political. In some instances, though by no means all, the courts reversed their convictions; but even that does not contradict the point, because in all such cases the court either held that proof of guilt was insufficient or that the law itself was so defective as to be unconstitutional—never that a valid law was not to be enforced if it was broken.

It is true that now and then in recent years some group of protestors that has seized a building (and thereby committed criminal trespass) has successfully insisted upon "amnesty" for themselves as one of the terms of their agreement to leave. Such an undertaking, however, is not a genuine example of amnesty, since the promise to waive prosecution was not uncoerced but was extorted as part of a bargaining process. And this alone would render such cases useless as an analogy to the situation of the Vietnam war draft-dodgers and deserters, for the latter are simply in no comparable position to bargain with the government.

THE GRAVITY OF THE OFFENSE. What really damages the case for regarding the draft-dodgers and deserters as mere practitioners of civil disobedience, however, or even for granting amnesty on the wider ground that many Americans share their view of the Vietnam war, is the gravity of their offense—a factor whose weight must be taken heavily into account, whatever exculpatory theory involving an act of grace is advanced on their behalf. These men did not merely seize a campus building for a week, or block traffic on Pennsylvania Avenue for an hour, or parade without a permit. By their actions, they irreparably injured many innocent people. It is to this aspect of the question of amnesty that we will now turn.

In our analysis of the respective rights and duties of a state and its citizens, we saw that despite the best will in the world a time may come when an individual feels bound in conscience to disobey a law enacted by the state. The state, in turn, is pragmatically justified in enforcing its laws, even upon such conscience-bound dissenters; and if its legislative procedures are democratic—i.e., if the dissenter had a fair opportunity to express his views and simply failed to prevail—the state's justification is not only pragmatic but moral. In such a case, the conscience-bound dissenter's only legitimate option is to disobey the law and pay the price. If he refuses to pay that price—e.g., by fleeing to Canada or Sweden, or simply by hiding—he may be prosecuted for his crime whenever he reappears in the United States.

The case for compassion and amnesty in such a situation obviously will depend in large part upon how seriously the crime of disobedience is regarded. Unfortunately for those draft-dodgers and deserters who seek amnesty today, I am afraid their crime is regarded very seriously indeed. And the reason is, I suspect, the same one that has historically prevented the United States from granting a general amnesty to draft-dodgers and deserters after its other wars.

Military action is one of the indispensable means whereby a state carries out its policies, and under modern conditions military service on the part of its young men is therefore one of the common requirements of any state, whether its legislative processes are democratic or not. Exemptions or postponements are sometimes permitted—as we saw in the case of the exemption of "conscientious objectors," and as in the case of educational deferments—but otherwise the basic obligation is, like any other law of the state, meant to be obeyed.

It is, after all, the pool of military manpower thus rendered available that defines in substantial part the military strength of the state. And it is therefore obvious, or ought to be, that any individual who, by dodging the draft or deserting the armed forces, arbitrarily removes himself from that manpower pool, is striking directly at the state's ability to implement its policies —perhaps, even, to survive.

True enough, the United States of America will undoubtedly survive the defection of Private Jones, and even continue to implement its policies by military means where necessary. But that is only because others will predictably step forward to fill the gap in the ranks created by Private Jones's departure. And that brings us to the ugliest consequence of this business of draft-dodging or deserting.

At any given moment, the manpower pool available to the United States government, to be drawn upon for its armed forces, is only a certain size. Depending upon the situation, the need to draw on it may be large or small. (At the moment it is small, and we are seeking to maintain the desired levels of personnel by strictly voluntary means; but a stand-by draft system remains on the books, and will assuredly be invoked whenever the military circumstances require it. Senator Hatfield and Mr. Schardt may deplore this if they wish; but the draft law can only be repealed by democratic processes, and thus far the political representatives of a majority of Americans have signally refused to remove it from the statute books.)

If, however, the draft is in force (as it was throughout the period of America's ground involvement in the Vietnam war), any individual who arbitrarily removes himself from the manpower pool inevitably redistributes its necessary burdens and risks among those remaining in the pool. The burden of service, the risk of injury, and even of death—all become heavier for those who remain, every time a member of the manpower pool crosses the border to sanctuary in Canada.

Let me illustrate this point with some concrete figures. Out of a total American population of about 200 million, the government had available, in the years 1962-1972—after excusing the true conscientious objectors and everyone else who had a lawful reason to be excused—a pool of about 10 million young men of appropriate age and physical qualifications (not including volunteers) on whom to draw for the military implementation of its policies in Vietnam. Roughly 2 million of these men were ultimately drafted to serve in the armed forces. Of these, some 600,000 were among the approximately 2½ million members of the armed forces who served in Vietnam at one time or another. (The balance were volunteers.) Tragically, as we know, approximately 46,000 Americans were killed by enemy action in Vietnam, and another 303,000 were wounded—some, in fact, crippled for life.

Now, according to the Department of Defense, slightly more than 15,000 of the 46,000 men killed by enemy action in Vietnam were draftees. And while a similar breakdown is not available for the 303,000 wounded, it is reasonable to assume that approximately the same ratio obtained: namely, 1 in 3. So roughly 100,000 of the wounded were also draftees. In terms of ratios, then, 1 out of every 39 draftees sent to Vietnam was killed by enemy action, and 1 out of every 6 was wounded.

Let us now take the figure of 200,000 (or 1 in 10 of the 2 million who were drafted) as representing the number of young men who dodged the draft or deserted the armed forces. (I realize that this figure is subject to dispute; but absolute precision is not important for our present purpose. Certainly 200,000 is not a wildly exaggerated estimate, on the basis of their own apologists' claims. Mr. Schardt, for example, as we have seen, puts the figure at 560,000.) Presumably 60,000 of these men would have been among the 600,000 draftees sent to Vietnam (using the same ratio—1 in 10—that they bore to the total number drafted.) Since they evaded the draft or deserted, 60,000 *more* men had to be sent to Vietnam in their stead. And since, as we have seen, 1 out of every 6 of the 600,000 draftees who served in Vietnam were wounded, and a further 1 out of 39 gave their lives, *it follows that the defection of those 60,000 draft-dodgers and deserters resulted in the deaths of at least 1,500 of their fellow Americans who would otherwise be alive today, and the wounding of 10,000 more.*

This is the scarifying arithmetic that makes the actions of the draft-dodgers and deserters seem especially repellent—especially culpable. It does not matter if some figure I have used is inaccurate in some particular; the situation is plain, whatever its details: *There are thousands of Americans dead and buried today, or maimed for life, who would have survived unscathed if those who dodged the draft or deserted had accepted their fair share of the risks implicit in service in the Vietnam war.* They chose not to do so. Let us assume that their choice was based, not simply on a high regard for their own skins, but on the loftiest moral objections to the particular war in question. If so, however, they could have elected to disobey the draft laws, serve their time in a federal prison, and walk out as free men. But they preferred Stockholm and Toronto, or life "underground" in America, and in those circumstances it is hard to see what compelling claim they have upon the clemency of the nation that had to draft other men to take the risks they refused to run.

One cannot, as I remarked earlier, help thinking that a similar process of reasoning has underlain the striking reluctance of earlier Presidents and Congresses to grant a general unconditional amnesty to those who dodged the draft or deserted in previous wars. Far from being among those types of crimes (notably political offenses) for which amnesty is peculiarly suited, draft-dodging and deserting have historically been regarded, probably for the reason I have just described, as particularly difficult to forgive or forget.

THE ATTITUDE OF THE OFFENDERS. A further consideration, bearing upon the posture America should adopt toward those who dodged the draft or deserted during the Vietnam war, is the present attitude of those for whom amnesty is sought.

That this should be a consideration, in determining whether or not to grant amnesty, is hardly a new proposition. President Washington's pardon for those who participated in the Whiskey Rebellion specifically excepted, as we have seen, those who "refused or neglected to give assurance of submission to laws of the United States." President Lincoln in 1862 directed the release of various political prisoners held in military custody "on their subscribing to a parole engaging them to render no aid or comfort to the enemies in hostility to the United States." Less than two years later, Lincoln granted full pardon to repenting Confederates, on condition that they subscribe to and "maintain . . . inviolate" a prescribed oath of loyalty to the United States — and four months later stressed that the pardon was applicable only to nonprisoner rebels who voluntarily took the oath "with the purpose of restoring peace and establishing the national authority." President Andrew Johnson followed Lincoln's lead, offering amnesty to former Confederates who took an *unqualified oath of allegiance* to the United States.

This concern as to the attitude of the offender seeking amnesty is surely understandable. If amnesty is essentially a political act, designed to cool the embers of a controversy largely past, there is obviously little sense in extending it to individuals whose only interest is in fanning the embers. How do the Vietnam draft-dodgers and deserters measure up, when judged by such a standard?

Here we are obviously dealing with a spectrum of attitudes. Unquestionably some draft-dodgers and deserters regret their actions, and would be ready to return to the United States and live normal, constructive lives here if they were amnestied unconditionally or even allowed to perform some kind of "alternative service." But, equally without question, many of these young men remain essentially rebellious—sure that they were right about Vietnam, positive that the American government was wrong, and (far more important) still defiantly hostile to the American society in general. Are these people ready to "give assurance of submission to laws of the United States?" Would they subscribe to and "maintain . . . inviolate" an unqualified oath of allegiance to this country? Even if we were not so square as to request one, may we feel reasonably confident that such submission and allegiance would be forthcoming if requested? Let us see.

"We are not criminals to be locked up by some military and civilian leaders who conceived and directed the genocidal Vietnam war. I reject their assertions that they can judge me," declared one anonymous deserter who is now a fugitive living "underground" in the United States, but who contrived to publish his views on the Op Ed page of the *New York Times* on February 28, 1973.

On the same page a draft-dodger named Tom Needham, now a journalist in Canada, put it this way: "It is a mockery for the perpetrators of inhuman crimes against innocent civilians (such as the Christmas destruction of Bach Mai hospital) to brand resisters as criminals and to demand that they pay a price of alternate service doing humanitarian work."

Both American and Canadian reporters, interviewing draft-dodgers and deserters now resident abroad, have found that similar attitudes are typical among the men they spoke to. Here is how James S. Lewis started his article from Toronto on the subject, which appeared in the *New York Post* on January 30, 1973:

> "Amnesty be damned," said draft dodger Allen Kazmer as he sat in his comfortable living room overlooking one of the city's many deep ravines.
>
> "The pompous American attitude that all war resisters just spend their time gazing longingly over the border, aching to live down there again, makes me sick."
>
> Kazmer, 31, fled from his native Detroit across the Ambassador Bridge to Windsor, Ontario, in his tiny

sports car with his wife, Karen, and their luggage in
April, 1968.

His army reserve unit, which he had joined to avoid
the regular army, had been called to active duty.

The Kazmers will be eligible for Canadian citizenship this summer and they have no doubt about applying. After all, their son, Aaron, 2½, is a native-born
Canadian.

And here is Margaret Daly, of the *Toronto Daily Star,* writing in the *Washington Post* for March 18, 1973:

"If amnesty were declared tomorrow," says David
Pacini, a 27-year-old draft evader from Cleveland, "I
suppose that would be nice because I could visit my
parents in case they got sick or something and couldn't
visit me. But that would be the only use I could ever see
for it."

. . . But so far as [the resisters] are concerned, an
amnesty, if ever declared, must be universal and unconditional. It must include draft evaders, deserters and
those serving prison sentences because of their opposition to the war.

Any amnesty that implied "forgiveness" on the part
of the U.S. government would be rejected by most of the
war resisters in Toronto, they say, because they don't feel
they've done anything to be forgiven for.

Much the same attitude was reported by William Borders
in a dispatch in the *New York Times* from Montreal dated No-
vember 14, 1972:

. . . as one deserter put it, expressing a prevailing
sentiment: "Why should I be concerned about amnesty?
I'm not the one who committed the crime."

Again and again, war resisters now abroad have insisted
that, if there is to be any amnesty whatever, it will have to be

unconditional, without any provision for "alternative service" or something of the sort. This was the point stressed by Anthony Astrachan of the *Washington Post* in his Toronto report dated February 21, 1972:

> Most of the Americans who fled to Canada to avoid serving in the Vietnam war reject the idea of conditional amnesty, according to recognized spokesmen and individual exiles interviewed here.
>
> The exiles also challenge the view of them that they believe the American establishment holds—of lonely, tearful waifs dreaming of the day they can once again set foot on American soil . . .
>
> Mickey Bickell, 26, of Clearwater, Fla., cautioned that despite the talk of staying here at least half of the exiles would go back if they had the chance.
>
> But the only chance they would recognize, most exiles interviewed agreed, would be an unconditional amnesty, covering draft-dodgers and deserters alike.
>
> The amnesty proposals made by Sen. Robert A. Taft (R-Ohio) and Rep. Edward I. Koch (D-N.Y.) cover only draft-dodgers. They would impose the condition of some "alternative service" to make up for the military commitments the exiles skipped. In the exiles' eyes, this is punishment instead of recognition of their early awareness of the wrongness of the war, an awareness they believe much of America has come to share.

This notion that draft-dodgers and deserters don't deserve punishment, or even amnesty, but rather some sort of apology from the American people and government is a theme that also appears repeatedly in *Newsweek*'s comprehensive report on the exiles in its issue for January 17, 1972:

> Most of the exiles themselves feel strongly that they have done nothing wrong. "It's not a question of the government forgiving us," contends Rick Thome, a deserter now living in Vancouver. "The United States has to be willing, for once, to admit it made a mistake."

And further on, *Newsweek* quotes Pat Cook, a twenty-five-year-old Marine deserter from Kansas:

> "Ninety-eight percent of the people up here just don't think they've done anything wrong," said Cook.

A few paragraphs later:

> "The pie-in-the-sky dream here is not amnesty," said John Phillips, a draft evader from tiny Algona, Iowa, "but getting a piece of cheap land, a farm. The whole amnesty thing is just a joke, and the three-year alternative service thing is a laugh." The hole in his boot was patched with adhesive tape, but Phillips, 26, is staying on in Toronto with his wife and year-old son Morgan. "It makes me sad to think that people in the States are working hard to get amnesty, because people up here aren't going to appreciate it," he said, "especially if there is some notion that they have to admit guilt. We aren't criminals. There is no guilt here."

The point was summed up in a paragraph near the end of the *Newsweek* story:

> According to Charles O. Porter, a former Oregon Congressman who heads Amnesty Now, a national coalition with some 300 members [sic], the only proper amnesty is one that "makes the moral point that our government was wrong and these young men were right. If this country were willing to make that point offically, it would clear the air and end a lot of the alienation."

As a matter of fact, any attempt to establish such a proposition would create far more dissension than it would silence—and properly so. But the point is that many draft-dodgers and deserters quite seriously demand such an admission as the price of their consent to return to the United States.

The general attitude is at least equally defiant among

American draft-dodgers and deserters in Sweden—as might be expected among refugees in a nation bitterly hostile to the U.S. policy in Vietnam. Following are the opening paragraphs of a dispatch from Stockholm by Frank Rosenow of the Associated Press, published in the *New York Post* on March 13, 1972:

> Leaders of American draft resisters and deserters who have found refuge in Sweden say promises of amnesty aren't enough to bring the colony home.
>
> "I'm not going back," said George Meals of Atlanta, Ga.
>
> Meals, 27, and others among the estimated 670 draft-dodgers and Army dropouts living in Sweden have discussed the amnesty projects under consideration in Congress. But they say they don't want forgiveness because they aren't the guilty ones in the Vietnam war.
>
> "Every American tax paying citizen is a criminal for paying taxes that provide for the Indochina war," said Meals.
>
> "If amnesty was offered today only about 200 of us would think about going back," said Roberto Argento, 26.

A year later Meals hadn't changed his mind, according to Takashi Oka, whose article for the *Christian Science Monitor* appeared in its February 21, 1973 issue:

> "We're not the criminals in this war," says George Meals, a recording engineer at the University of Stockholm. George came to Sweden from an Army camp in Georgia five years ago. He admits he occasionally misses his home city, Atlanta, and says he would "probably go back" if granted an unconditional amnesty. "But I don't think we committed any crimes, and I'm not going to crawl and beg."

The crawling and begging, apparently, will have to be done by the people and government of the United States. A far cry

ndeed from the strict terms laid down by Washington, Lincoln
and Andrew Johnson!

The truth is that the draft-dodging and deserting that went
on during the Vietnam war were in many cases symptomatic, not
merely of the resister's aversion to the U.S. military role in Vietnam, but of his profound alienation from the traditions, values
and general direction of the American society.

Anthony Astrachan, in the *Washington Post* article already
quoted, detected such an attitude among many of those he interviewed:

> They are in no hurry to return home, the exiles
> insist—not only because the current amnesty proposals
> are unacceptable, but also because many of them reject
> the whole U.S. system, not just the Vietnam war.

Such total alienation from what might broadly be called
"the American life-style" has never been wholly absent from our
history, and probably never will be; no society could possibly
hope to please everyone born into it. Mr. Schardt professes to
fear that "America—a nation which has always been the beneficial recipient of waves of dissenters from repressive societies—
has changed so drastically that *we* are now the one forcing *our*
dissenters into permanent exile." But this does less than justice
to the historical record. From Thoreau and Lafcadio Hearn to
the many thousands of Americans who over the years have
chosen to live in Paris or elsewhere in Europe, the criticism of
America's alleged "materialism," of the cult of the go-getter, of
the Puritan work ethic, and of much else besides, has flourished,
and voluntary expatriation has been common.

Many of the draft-dodgers and deserters display a striking
similarity to this familiar pattern. In the 1960s, spurred by a
decline in religious faith, the loosening of family bonds, constant TV exposure to exotic life-styles and numerous other stim-
uli (not least the all-too-visible horrors of war, as relentlessly
reported from Vietnam), their revulsion against "Amerika"

formed itself into what was hailed, somewhat misleadingly, as a whole "counterculture," complete with its own distinctive styles in clothing, hairdos, music, drugs, sexual attitudes, family organization, etc.

Not surprisingly, this new movement soon developed an equally distinctive political viewpoint. Despite a deceptive patina of borrowed Marxist rhetoric about "capitalistic exploitation," etc., the political orientation of the "counterculture" was actually neo- (and ultra-) libertarian. "The Establishment"—meaning the whole organization of social life in the United States—was condemned. Government, business, social institutions, and social conventions in general, were denounced. Life was to be lived more simply—perhaps, even, primitively.

In this Rousseau-like dream of the future there were certain tendencies which have had a positive and even healthy effect on contemporary American politics: the growing concern over pollution of the environment, for one thing (and up to a point) and the salutary and much-belated fear of big government, for another. But despite these constructive aspects, the basic political thrust of the "counterculture" has been profoundly negative and bitterly hostile to American society in general. By the mid 1960s, it had fastened onto the Vietnam war as its particular bête noire—no doubt partly because the draft directly threatened so many young men who were bent on "dropping out" of the American society, but also because the war inevitably threw into high relief precisely those aspects of American life to which the "counterculture" objected most strenuously. Here, they were told by their own propagandists, was a huge government, conspiratorially entangled with a bunch of greedy corporations (some manufacturing weapons of war, and the rest no doubt intent on exploiting the peoples and resources of Southeast Asia), mobilizing the manpower and wealth of the United States to impose its will by force on a small nation of brown-skinned people ten thousand miles away. Most of us would probably not consider that a very fair description of the Vietnam war, but that is unquestionably the way it was regarded by much of the political left, and above all by the members of the youthful "counter-culture."

In such circumstances, it is hardly surprising that scores or hundreds of thousands of young men dodged the draft or deserted the armed forces, and that they "are in no hurry to return home . . . because many of them reject the whole U.S. system, not just the Vietnam war." To such people, an offer of "amnesty" would naturally seem ludicrous at best and insulting at worst. Many of them are political activists, however, and these would see in such an amnesty a golden opportunity to return to the United States and escalate their private war against the hated "System." Precisely to the extent that they are *not* to be regarded as ordinary criminals, but as political zealots, such people fall squarely within the categories specifically *excluded* from the amnesties proclaimed by Washington and Lincoln: namely, persons who "refused or neglected to give assurance of submission to the laws of the United States," and who refused to take an oath of loyalty "with the purpose of restoring peace and establishing the national authority."

Of course, not all draft-dodgers and deserters have such a fundamentally rebellious point of view. As noted earlier, we are dealing with a broad spectrum of attitudes. Among the exiles and those "underground," there must be many who, as confused or frightened teenagers, were pressured into draft-dodging or deserting by misguided parents, leftist teachers or domineering contemporaries. Now that they are older and American ground participation in the Vietnam war has ended, such young men may see matters very differently indeed. Even if they are not to be excused from all punishment whatever, they certainly deserve to be treated far more gently than the fiery rebels. *And that is precisely why amnesty, or any other approach to the problem of draft-dodgers and deserters that treats them all alike, is so strik-*

ingly inappropriate. Fortunately the normal processes of American justice are highly flexible, and can make all the needful distinctions. It is to this point that we shall turn in closing.

The Options Available under the Law

While it is true that a state will normally seek to punish a person who breaks its laws, there is necessarily, and quite properly, a great deal of flexibility in the actual process of law enforcement. In what follows, I shall be assuming that a law (either the draft law or the law against desertion) has been broken, that there is technically sufficient concrete evidence to support a conviction, and that the law violator either has been caught or has turned himself over to the authorities.

The first point at which any mitigating circumstances are normally taken into account is when the public prosecutor looks over the case with a view to deciding whether it should be prosecuted at all. He is, of course, sworn to enforce the laws, and it would not be proper for him to overlook a serious crime merely out of some sort of obscure sympathy for the criminal. But "prosecutorial discretion" is a very real discretion nonetheless, and it is exercised—in favor of not prosecuting—every day. The prosecutor is entitled to consider whether a jury would be willing to convict, in the light of all the circumstances; what the effect of aroused public passions, one way or the other, might be; and in general whether prosecution and conviction, in this particular case, would be in the best interests of society as a whole. He would also be at liberty to consider all of the distinctions so carefully drawn by Senator Hatfield: between draft-dodgers and deserters; between draft-dodgers who fled to Canada and those who failed to report for induction but stayed here; between deserters who deserted in this country and those who deserted under combat conditions in Vietnam; and so on.

It is certainly reasonable to assume that at least some draft-dodgers, if not deserters, would be spared any prosecution whatever, by reason of the exercise of prosecutorial discretion.

Moreover, after an indictment has been decided upon and obtained, prosecutors will often try to ascertain—if only to avoid the trouble and expense of a trial—whether the defendant would be willing to plead guilty in return for a recommendation of a relatively mild penalty.

But let us suppose that the defendant is tried and duly convicted. It is now up to the trial judge to determine what sentence he shall receive: whether a fine, or imprisonment, or both; if a fine, how large it shall be; if a prison term, how long. He also has the option of suspending the sentence he imposes, in whole or in part. The trial judge is in a particularly good position to make these decisions. He has watched the unfolding of the evidence; he has heard the arguments for both sides; if the defendant has testified, the judge has had an opportunity to form his own estimate of the man: his strengths, his weaknesses, and the likelihood that he will be a law-abiding citizen hereafter. The judge will also have available to him, in almost every case, the defendant's previous criminal record, if any, as well as the reports of psychologists, social workers, parole officials and others who have had an opportunity to study and assess the defendant as an individual. The judge is at perfect liberty to impose any sentence he believes is called for, from the statutory maximum to none at all.

It is at this point, I believe, that we can feel reasonably sure that the necessary distinctions will be made between hot-eyed zealots implacably hostile to their country and impressionable young men who were too easily misled by others. Let us assume, however, that the draft-dodger or deserter has been convicted and sentenced, that the conviction has been upheld on appeal, and that the sentence is a harsh one. There still remains the final, classic resort of one too severely penalized: executive clemency. This is one of the oldest prerogatives of sovereignty: the right of a king, or (nowadays) his republican surrogate, to reduce a sentence, or indeed to pardon a criminal altogether.

In the case of such federal crimes as draft-dodging and deserting, the prerogative belongs to the President. To him or his representatives will be forwarded the record of the trial, the decisions of the trial judge and the appellate courts, and all collateral materials bearing upon the case. An appeal to executive clemency is precisely *not* addressed, at least ordinarily, to the question of the defendant's technical guilt or innocence, but to the over-all equities of the situation. If there is anything at all to be said, in extenuation of the defendant's actions or in protest against the sentence imposed on him, it will be said and considered here. Here, supremely, is the place for that "moderation and tenderness" of which President Washington spoke, and which Mr. Schardt tries to coopt as an argument for a blanket amnesty.

In the case of Vietnam war resisters, it would probably be advisable for the President, if they come forward in substantial numbers, to follow the precedent of President Truman after World War II and appoint a board to advise him on the exercise of clemency in these cases. In that way, defendants with cases of roughly equal merit could be sure of equal treatment. To ease the burden on the courts, it might even be possible for the amnesty board (or boards), working within guidelines laid down by the President, to recommend nonprosecution in certain types of cases and light sentences in others, and thus further equalize the policies of different jurisdictions.

In place of this truly impressive structure of orderly justice —soberly invoked, meticulously applied, carefully reviewed and tinctured with compassion—the advocates of amnesty would impose a single monolithic rule: *Every* draft-dodger and deserter must go scot-free, or at worst (as under the Hatfield proposal) throw himself on the mercy of some special tribunal charged with absolving him if it can detect, in his conduct, the slightest hint of serious moral or political protest.

Nothing could be more unfair. A general and unconditional amnesty would treat alike young men whose only mistake may have been to place the commands of their parents above those of their country, and professional revolutionaries whose only reason for wanting to come home is that they can damage

America more effectively from within. Moreover, under the Hatfield "compromise" the latter might actually fare better than the former, since their conduct was at least politically motivated.

And while we are on the subject of fairness, just how fair would an amnesty be to those who, while equally unable as a matter of conscience to obey the draft law, were unlucky enough to get caught, or simply honorable enough and brave enough to stay in this country and openly accept the prescribed legal penalty for breaking it? Shall the terms they served in prison brand them forever as "suckers," compared to the cool calculators in Toronto and Stockholm who were clever enough—and (a point often overlooked) prosperous enough—to make themselves scarce until the war was over and their apologists back home could launch a drive for amnesty?

In the long run, I am afraid, the continued struggle for amnesty will only lengthen, and perhaps perpetuate, the exile of those young men among the draft-dodgers and deserters who otherwise could soon resume constructive lives in the United States. For it will encourage them to hope that there is, or soon will be, an easier way out than coming home and accepting whatever punishment is deemed to be their due. In that hope, I believe, they are tragically mistaken.

It is not wise to speak too confidently about the future. But if the 200-year record of the American attitude toward amnesty for wartime draft-dodgers and deserters has any meaning today, this country will be very reluctant indeed to permit the Vietnam specimens of the breed to surface or come home without *some* appropriate legal penalty. Too many husbands, fathers, brothers and sons who had to take their places in the armed forces are dead today, or injured, or were at a minimum gravely inconvenienced in their careers and family lives, as a result of their defection.

We are not, after all, demanding anything that could conceivably be described as cruel or unusual. Mr. Schardt pleads that "Americans do not believe in permanently destroying other people or making them suffer forever"—but who is demanding any such thing? There is no question of a death penalty here, or of perpetual involuntary exile, or even (save perhaps in the most aggravated cases) of any very lengthy prison sentence. All these young men are being required to do is submit themselves to the ordinary judicial processes of this country, and accept the ordinary penalties, in connection with laws they consciously and very deliberately broke.

If, however, some of them remain unwilling to abide by the laws of the United States, and to accept punishment for the ones they have broken, they are free to live elsewhere. In that case, one can only hope that Canada and Sweden may, in time, find them better citizens than they proved to be of the land where they were born.

AMNESTY?

IF...

Mark O. Hatfield

October 26, 1945
Anchored Dason Point
Haiphong, Indo-China

Dear Folks:

 Here we are in Indo-China adding another spot on the globe to my world travels. We anchored about 1000 (10 o'clock) in the muddy water off Dason Point. Very shortly our ship was surrounded with native boats begging for food and clothes. It was sickening to see the absolute poverty and the rags these people are in. We thought the Philippines were in a bad way, but they are wealthy compared to these exploited people. The Philippines were in better shape before the war, but the people here have never known anything but squalor since the French heel has been on them.

 Again, on the beach, we were sickened by the sight of the poverty of the natives. It is just like Willkie said in his One World—*you see the mansion on top of the hill with the many shacks surrounding it. I tell you, it is a crime the way we occidentals have enslaved these people in our mad desire for money. The French seem to be the worst and are followed pretty closely by the Dutch and the English. I can certainly see why these people don't want us to return and continue to spit upon them. There is so much constructive work that could be done here in the Orient and sometimes I get the urge to come out here and do something . . . . .*

   All my love,

   Mark

In 1945 I was still serving with the U.S. Navy in Asia, even though the war with Japan had ended. We had been sent up to Indochina to transport some of Chiang Kai-shek's troops back into battle during the Chinese civil war. Our ship laid anchor in Haiphong, and later we went inland to Hanoi.

With their defeat, the Japanese occupation of Indochina had ended. The nationalistic fervor of the Vietnamese had been united under Ho Chi Minh, whom the United States had assisted in the mutual struggle against the Japanese. In Hanoi, he and his followers proclaimed the Democratic Republic of Vietnam with a declaration of Vietnam's independence on September 2, 1945, believing that their decades of struggle against colonialism had finally been victorious. It became perfectly obvious to me, and to others in Indochina during that period, that Ho Chi Minh and the Vietminh were widely accepted by the Vietnamese as their authentic nationalistic leadership. The Communist ideology held by Ho and his comrades didn't compromise their nationalistic, anticolonial commitment. To the Vietnamese, Ho Chi Minh was a genuine hero, leader and liberator.

What made an even deeper impression on me during those days was the suffering and deprivation of the people of Vietnam. The sight of starving, malnourished children, and Vietnamese women searching frantically for scraps of food for their families, was burned into my memory. The Vietnamese had been victimized by unbearable suffering—suffering that had come at the hands of one foreign occupier after another. They wanted their liberation because they wanted to eat, to survive, to be free from such foreign oppression. Nationalism was not just an appealing ideological, political ideal; it grew out of the hunger of their empty stomachs, the pain of their tortured bodies and the anguish of their dehumanized lives.

I returned home from the war never believing that the suffering of the Vietnamese had only begun, and never imagining that those memories would thrust me headlong into a wrenching political struggle opposing my own country's intervention in Indochina two decades later.

When the French returned to Indochina in 1946 I was shocked and depressed. The war that followed seemed inevitable; our growing assistance to the French in that war seemed unforgivable. When the elections promised by the Geneva Accords of 1954 failed to materialize, U.S. policy became more questionable, especially when the rationale for our position against elections was revealed to be that Ho Chi Minh was so popular.

Our growing involvement with the Diem regime in Southern Vietnam during the years that followed, and our insistence that there were two countries in Vietnam, appeared, in my mind at least, to be mistaken and almost indefensible. The various governments to succeed each other in the South after World War II had no legitimate and broad nationalistic appeal. First they were the puppets for the French, and later they were becoming the vassals of American policy and power.

All these impressions had remained more or less in the back of my mind during these years. After all, the events in Indochina were generally regarded as inconsequential history in a remote corner of the world. But then, as American soldiers began going to Vietnam to fight, the memories of those days in Haiphong began coming back more frequently.

The entire mood of the country during the early 1960s, however, made it difficult to judge our involvement in Indochina on the basis of memories from the 1940s. Americans were being sent overseas to defend our "national interest," to keep our "commitments," and to oppose "aggression." Once Americans were in battle on foreign soil, the American people instinctively believed that they were there for righteous and just purposes. It was nearly heretical to seriously suggest in those days that we were intervening in what was essentially a civil war, and that we were choosing the unpopular side. The impulse of defending our nation's honor made it difficult to even conceive that our intervention in Indochina might be a dishonorable, immoral mistake.

By 1966 this all came to a decisive confrontation for me.

I was ending my second term as Governor of Oregon. Two years earlier, at the Republican National Convention, I had said in the keynote address: "Time and again this administration has revealed distrust of us all. Why, why do they fear telling the American people what our foreign policy is? Even when American boys are dying in a war without a name." The next year, after President Johnson was reelected and the little war he promised to end was escalated, the Governors were briefed by the White House and asked to support the President. I said no to a nearly unanimous voice vote in support of the resolution to back President Johnson at the 1965 Governors' Conference. All this set the stage for the Governors' Conference in 1966.

The war had escalated far more seriously by July of that year. On the eve of the conference, there were more White House briefings. The President was anxious to demonstrate that the nation's Governors backed his policies in Southeast Asia. Politically, the situation was complicated by the fact that I was a candidate for the United States Senate that year. To defy the President and rebuke the nation's commitment to Vietnam, I was told, would amount to political suicide. In my mind, I had even constructed the reasons, and rationale, why I could support the resolution to be offered to the Governors for approval. That course of action seemed both necessary and explicable. It could be justified and defended, with good reason. But inner self rebelled against such a choice. I am dwelling with what went on within me during that time because it is the best way to reveal the growth of my convictions and feelings about the war. Pascal says that "The heart has its reason which reason cannot understand." Ultimately, it was not the carefully reasoned arguments about strategy and foreign policy that solidified my oppostion to the war. Rather, it was the deeper spiritual urgings that compelled my actions. That best explained the lone vote against the resolutions at that Governors'

Conference and the many acts which followed. I sensed that I could not live with myself any other way.

At its root, I felt it all was a moral issue. What we were doing in Indochina seemed terribly mistaken, and wrong. The rational reasons why that was so were much harder to articulate then. To suggest at that time that your nation was morally wrong in a war it was fighting, with dead Americans coming home each day, seemed pretentious and utterly disloyal, especially when there was no way to condone or defend the morality of the other side's tactics. So the discussion, and the questioning of White House advisers, invariably centered on diplomatic, strategic and political considerations. But the best defense for my convictions went back to the memories of the time I had spent in Indochina, and the feelings I had then. In light of that, I saw what America had come to do in Indochina as unnecessary, unjust and immoral.

As the war escalated and public awareness expanded, the symptoms of immorality began to become more and more apparent. The body counts, the refugees, the bombing, the civilian casualties, the free-fire zones, the search and destroy missions, the napalm—these all revealed a callousness toward the sanctity of human life that was frightening. Even those disposed to believe that this war was a just war found it increasingly more difficult to reconcile such brutal means with the ends that were being sought. Gradually, a moral abhorrence of the war became grounded in those who opposed Johnson's and then Nixon's policies in Indochina.

When Richard Nixon became President, and his secret plan for ending the war seemed only to prolong it, I had decided to vote against every appropriation bill containing any money to support the war effort, despite what else the bill might fund. It was impossible to approve funds for policies that I believed to be immoral. The President's invasion of Cambodia in 1970 galvanized a concerted congressional effort to cut off the funds for the war. The first McGovern-Hatfield amendment was introduced at the time of the Cambodian invasion, which proved to be only the start of persistent efforts that have continued over the past three years to stop appropriating money for the war.

By April of 1971, the insistence that Congress must not pay for the war had pushed me into wrestling with a deeper, more personal dilemma: Could I, as a citizen, justify paying for the war? I had just figured out my federal taxes, and then calculated how much money I was contributing personally to the war I believed to be immoral. What ensued were days of deep personal conflict, and the searching of my conscience. I recognized that I was bound also by my oath of office as a United States Senator; I had pledged to uphold and defend the Constitution, and that included the Sixteenth Amendment. Further, I learned that Christians in the early church who refused service in the Roman legions did faithfully pay their taxes. One alternative I considered was placing that portion of my taxes that would pay for the war in escrow, pending a court determination regarding the constitutionality of the war. But that option seemed weak and transparent since I knew that the courts were extremely unlikely ever to make such a determination. From the time I had first set anchor at Haiphong, through the day I knew I would oppose American policies that were, in my judgment, immoral, I had been brought to confront the personal consequences of those convictions.

From this struggle of conscience, I determined that the law and the Constitution, which I was sworn to uphold, demanded and deserved first my allegiance. The immorality of the war policy could be changed only through the law and the constitutional system, despite the abridgements of that system by the Executive. My first responsibility was to commit myself more deeply than ever to the restoration of our constitutional ideals, attempting to persuade my colleagues to stop voting for money to continue the war. Two months later, the Senate voted on the second McGovern-Hatfield amendment; we fell short again, but had picked up three votes. Now forty-two Senators favored this approach, and only a week later, forty-nine Senators voted for another fund cut-off, one short of a majority of voting Senators.

I have begun by sharing in depth the evolution of my convictions about the war because that is where we must inevitably start in considering amnesty. Our views on amnesty will necessarily be molded by these convictions.

It is obvious that the current sentiment in the country against amnesty stems from the deep desire to believe our nation has done no wrong. We want desperately to believe that our peace has brought honor. No nation ever wants to admit that it may have been wrong. We would rather believe that our country stands beyond the reach of such judgment. But we will not be able to rewrite history, suppressing the truth from ourselves.

Sooner or later, I believe the nation will come to accept at least the moral ambiguity of our involvement in Indochina, if not the outright culpability of some of our actions. We will come to acknowledge that every step we take in the world is not morally invincible. I believe that most Americans sense at one level the truth about Vietnam; we do not have an easy conscience about this chapter of our history. But as with any tinge of guilt, our tendency is to repress it, and divert ourselves away from recognizing its presence. Repression of guilt is never a very healthy act. It makes us self-righteous, and defensive. Unwilling to admit the possibility of error, we are unable to learn from our history, to mature and to be redeemed. Our faults remain with us, and become even more dangerous because they escape acknowledgment. With time we will be able to bear more of the truth, and recognize where we were wrong. That does not mean there ever will be, or need be, a strong consensus that sees the war as a total moral travesty, and cries out for expiation. Rather, I believe there will emerge to the surface of the American conscience a clear sense that our involvement in Indochina was mistaken, got out of hand, and raised questions about our national character. The truth, in my judgment, may go even deeper than that, but at least this much will become clear to many. Then it will become untenable to make self-righteous denunciations of those who refused to accept America's policies. Then there can emerge a spirit of tolerance and reconciliation, based on a recognition of the nation's fallibility. What we must reject, then, is the urge toward national vindication that appears so tempting. The idea that we can achieve national "honor" out of this nightmare of moral agony is a threatening, dangerous illusion that must be decisively discarded. The greatest injury to America's spirit would be for us to forget the tragedy of the Indochina experience by blinding ourselves to our own capacity for self-deception, aggrandizement, and senseless inhumanity.

We need a spirit of repentance in our land. I realize that may be far too much to ask, or expect. Yet the thought of turning our national attention, at appropriate times, to the need for repentance should not be foreign to us. Abraham Lincoln did so. He had a profound sense of how the nation stood under judgment for its actions. Though committed to the justice of his cause, he also knew that he was not the one to make the ultimate judgments of history. President Lincoln specifically called the entire nation, North and South, to times of national humiliation and repentance. His Proclamation of a Day of Humiliation, Fasting, and Prayer on April 30, 1863, reads:

> Whereas, it is the duty of nations, as well as of men, to owe their dependence upon the overruling power of God, to confess their sins and transgressions, in humble sorrow, we have become too self-sufficient to feel the necessity of redeeming and preserving grace, too proud to pray to the God that made us.
>
> It behooves us, then to humble ourselves before the offended Power, to confess our national sins, and to pray for clemency and forgiveness.

Realistically it may be imprudent and impractical to expect such a spirit of repentance to develop amongst the American people today. Calls to repentance are always sounded far more frequently than they are heeded.

But it is not too much to expect a spirit of humility, tolerance and reconciliation to develop. That does not require the admission that we may have been wrong. It only requires the very human recognition that we should temper our convictions about who was right with the acknowledgment of our mutual fallibility. By first nurturing this simple and humane spirit in our land, we can then rightly approach the question of amnesty.

One's beliefs regarding amnesty will also be molded by one's convictions concerning the military draft. We must remember that the war in Indochina was fought without a declaration of war ever being passed by the Congress. Yet thousands of young Americans were forced by military conscription to risk their lives in Southeast Asia.

Had the constitutionality of the war never been in doubt, and had the Congress duly authorized our massive intervention, then one could build a justification for relying on a military draft to carry out the nation's clear-cut commitment to war. But such was never the case with the Vietnam war. The Congress and the nation were never really given the opportunity to choose whether or not to become involved. We suddenly found ourselves more and more deeply enmeshed in a war that seemed to have no beginning and that could not be stopped or ended.

Such an undeclared war was possible, in large part, because of the existence of a peacetime draft. Conscription without war had never existed until World War II. Until then, a draft was instituted only after the Congress had chosen to commit the nation to war. Then, conscription had always ended with the conclusion of the war. But when the option for intervention in Vietnam developed, the military draft was already in operation. The Executive had at its disposal the capacity to conscript all the men they needed. Just as the Congress, and the people, were never given a clear choice whether or not to enter into war, they were also denied the choice whether to institute a system of conscription that would send men off to fight and die in that war. Therefore, if one opposed conscription as a matter of principle, as I do, there was all the more reason to be against a draft that had been initiated in peacetime and then used to support an undeclared war. Our thinking about conscription, and its place in American society, should be informed and influenced by our history.

For most of our nation's 200-year history, military conscription has been rightly viewed as alien to the principles of democracy and a free society. The threat of conscription brought many of the original settlers to America, and was a factor in two of the nation's earliest wars—the Revolutionary War and the War of 1812. Although the colonies had hundreds of conscription laws that dealt with specific requirements for service, provided for exemptions and penalties, and laid down procedures, the colonial militias consisted primarily of volunteers. Those that were inducted usually served no more than three months, and that in a part-time capacity similar to that of reservists today. The Revolutionary War, therefore, was fought almost entirely with volunteers recruited by a bounty system into the state militias or the Continental Army.

In 1790 Congress rejected Secretary of War Knox's proposal for a combination of universal militia service and a federal draft, perhaps mindful of Benjamin Franklin's argument against British impressment of colonists into His Majesty's Navy.

America's army was so undermanned and so often defeated in the War of 1812 that Congress fiercely debated and finally passed a modified draft making extensive use of enlistment bonuses, or bounties, but the war had ended by the time passage was secured. The Mexican War was easily handled by the small standing army, so the issue of conscription did not arise again until 1863, when President Lincoln asked Congress for authority to conscript men to supplement the one million who had answered the original call to arms. When Congress enacted the necessary legislation, riots erupted in New York City that left a thousand dead. Lincoln had his draft, but it was apparent that strong opposition to military conscription remained. With the conclusion of the war the draft was ended.

Congress acted swiftly when faced with the need for men in the next major war. Immediately after the declaration of war in 1917, Congress passed a comprehensive draft law, thus precluding reliance on volunteers.

Despite inequities in the draft law, and the fact that this was the first time men had been conscripted to serve overseas, opposition to the 1917 draft was not nearly so violent as the response to the Civil War act. In large part this was due to the deep sense of national unity and support for the war effort. Evasion replaced open violence, however, and more than 250,000 men failed to report for induction. And once again, with the war's end came conscription's end.

The new war in Europe prompted Congress to enact another draft law on September 14, 1940, before our actual entry into the war. Debate was heated. Senator Arthur Vandenberg assailed the peacetime draft as "repugnant to the spirit of democracy and the soul of Republican institutions." He also saw the dangers of justifying conscription in the name of freedom:

> . . . the very conditions with which the world confronts us today—the ruthless destruction of personal liberty under a dozen flags, the rape of civil freedom to the west and to the east, the challenges in behalf of [enacting conscription]—all these really are reasons why we should be doubly jealous of the American way of life, rather than being excuses why we should hastily abandon it.

Senator Robert Taft, characteristically, was more blunt:

> It is said that a compulsory draft is a democratic system. I deny that it has anything to do with democracy . . . It is far more typical of totalitarian nations than of democratic nations. The theory behind it leads directly to totalitarianism. It is absolutely opposed to the principles of individual liberty which have always been considered part of American democracy. . . . The principle of a compulsory draft is basically wrong.

Despite the protestations of these and other members of Congress, the draft law passed easily. A little more than a year later Pearl Harbor put an end to most dissent on the issue. The Selective Service System established a structure of deferments and exemptions that remained virtually intact until recent years, and the draft managed to win grudging acceptance if not overwhelming support.

The draft was allowed to expire on March 31, 1947, in the tradition of postwar demobilization, after requirements for replacements and occupational armies had been met. But the Army immediately expressed concern that it would be unable to maintain the force levels it claimed were required.

President Truman rose to the occasion in 1948 with a proposal for universal military training, but Congress instead renewed the old draft law. At the height of the Korean War in 1951, Congress passed a four-year extension of the Selective Service System, and the draft became an accepted fixture of American life.

As such, Congressional extension of the Universal Military Service and Training Act in 1955, 1959 and 1963 generated little debate and virtually no opposition. Looking over the record of the draft debates since World War II, there are very few statements dealing with the basic assumption of a peacetime military draft, its domestic and foreign implications, and, most importantly, its implications for the individual in our society. The earlier warnings of Senators Taft and Vandenberg were overwhelmed by cold war rhetoric and the "America first" statism evident in President Kennedy's famous "ask what you can do for your country."

It is my conviction that a compulsory draft is alien to our principles of freedom. Those principles are not merely a part of our democracy, but its very foundation.

The central issue is the meaning of a free society and the institutions we create to insure the maximum freedom of choice for each individual. This, coupled with a deep distrust of centralized governmental power, were the cornerstones of our Declaration of Independence and the Constitution. The Selective Service System is a prime example of centralized governmental power that severely limits an individual's freedom, for it can take him from his home and against his will place him in the armed forces under circumstances where he may well lose his life.

In essence, conscription is a form of involuntary servitude. We theoretically abolished slavery after the War Between the States. That form of slavery was a form of economic servitude. We subsequently instituted an even more onerous form—military conscription—and rationalized it by saying it would enhance our freedoms at home and enable us to create freedom abroad. But we cannot try to defend freedom at home or create it abroad by taking it away from our own citizens—we cannot export what we do not have.

To attempt to do so is a contradiction of our 200-year history as a free nation. It was the contradiction of those ideals about freedom and liberty that has given us the dilemma of what to do about amnesty. We must recognize the severity of choices faced by young men who were morally opposed to the war. They had to reconcile their duty to country with their duty to conscience.

The choices they faced often became desperate. They could attempt to achieve status as conscientious objectors to all war, if that conformed to their beliefs and if they met the requirements determined by the Selective Service Board. If this failed or was not possible, then they could choose to move to Canada or elsewhere, or to go to jail, or to kill men they did not hate in a war they could not justify for a cause they did not believe in.

Because of the cases of men caught in such moral dilemma that I personally was aware of, I set as my first legislative priority in the Senate the end to the draft, and establishment of an all-volunteer military. Each year during my first six-year term this issue was considered and debated, until the use of the draft was ended at the beginning of 1973. The Selective Service System has remained intact, however, with its apparatus for draft registration. Congress still must repeal the Military Selective Service Act in order to eliminate the structure and apparatus used for military conscription. As one who consistently fought the existence of the draft as an unjust institution, then, I feel an affinity toward those who faced trials of conscience and decision under the brunt of conscription. I believe they were being forced to make choices that the government never should have demanded of them.

The rights of life, liberty and the pursuit of happiness are not rights granted to man by government. Rather, they are inalienable rights "endowed by our Creator." They are God-given rights.

Any proposals for compulsory "national service" would only injure, rather than preserve, these rights. I believe deeply in the need to serve one's country. But a country is more than its government; it is the people. By serving the needs of others, and by involving ourselves in solving local problems, we are rendering true service to our country. Such authentic service can never be compelled. It must be motivated by the simple willingness to meet needs, serve others, and help one's fellow man. Here will lie the true strength of our nation: it will be measured by the voluntary willingness of our citizens to give for the sake of giving to the well-being of each other and all society.

I have tried to express fully my views about our involvement in Vietnam and my thoughts about the draft. Convictions on these issues will shape one's approach to the question of amnesty, and have strongly influenced my thinking. I believe that our involvement in Indochina was tragically misguided and immoral. I believe that the conscription for that war was an unjust infringement upon the most fundamental rights of the citizen. Therefore, my disposition is to be generous, sympathetic, and comprehensive in granting amnesty to those who held similar convictions, but went to jail, left the country, or are culpable under the demands of the law in other ways for the sake of their beliefs.

Any disposition to be generous about amnesty, however, must immediately confront the sanctity of the rule of law.

Our government, we trust, is a government of law, and not of men. All the virtues, values, guarantees and benefits in a democracy rest upon fundamental respect for the law. The law is the vehicle for translating our ideals into reality. It is the law which makes justice possible. If the law's ability to command and receive the natural respect of the citizenry erodes, then the total foundation of government is put under siege. Even a government with the most just and virtuous policies would be meaningless if its citizens felt no duty to adhere to the law.

The most revolutionary dimension of our nation's founding was the enshrinement of the belief that law could more justly govern the affairs of men than men could. People were given the right and power of self-government through the legislature— the lawmaking body. Its law would rule on the behalf of all the people, and over them all, unlike government by the whims and wishes of princes, monarchs and despots.

The idea was a radical one. Skeptics thought that people could never be loyal and respectful to a mere process of decision-making, as they were to a monarch. What, after all, would hold such a government together? What would prevent a hectic state of anarchy, where each man followed his opinion rather than abide by the decisions that were made after heated controversy, but then applied to all? What would insure that the losers would adhere to decisions after exercising such strong rights to oppose their adoption?

The only contrary argument to be offered by those who believed in the experiment of democracy was that the process of lawmaking, and the constitutional structure to guide it, would win the allegiance that previously was asked for only by kings. The whole venture rested on a faith that law, justly and democratically made, would come to achieve an inviolate sanctity.

In constructing the separation of powers, the framers of the Constitution attempted to insure democracy's durability by providing permanent means for continuous, and even revolutionary, change. No one man would ever have the power to impose his will arbitrarily on the people. One always had recourse to the law, and the law could always be changed. Therefore, one's disagreement with specific laws need not compromise one's allegiance to the rule of law, for one was guaranteed the right to influence and be represented in the making of law.

For two hundred years, our democracy has responded to the persistent revolutionary impulses in our land, and accommodated them by continual, often radical political change. We never had any guarantee that our system would be perpetually responsive, resilient and vibrant, adjusting to inevitable change while preserving its original ideals. The process of American democracy has continued only because enough citizens have believed they had the right, the privilege and the potential access to political power. They believed that they could make a difference in their society. Moreover, they believed in protecting and preserving those rights. So allegiance was placed in the process and the possibilities of democracy, and firm adherence was given to the law as the instrument of government.

I am not about to maintain that we have embodied the

ideals of justice and liberty that lie at the foundation of our democracy. In fact, I have argued strenuously for nearly the past decade that the war in Indochina, the draft and the power of the Executive have made unprecedented assaults upon the viability of those ideals. We have witnessed, in many ways, the total contravention of those ideals by our pursuit of the Indochinese war, by the infringements upon our domestic freedoms and by the idolatry of presidential power. Because of these and other tragic realities of American life, I cannot contend that our government has always embodied, in reality, our democratic ideals, or that the law, in its present expression, has insured justice and liberty for all citizens.

But those ideals still exist. The force of the protest against their abridgement is a sign that those ideals are a live and vital force, powerful enough to impel unquenchable political pressure demanding their restoration. The rule of law, and process of law, still merit our resolute allegiance precisely because these remain the means for overcoming the distortion, manipulation and violation of lawful principles and constitutional ideals.

Such a fundamental allegiance to the rule of law was what enabled President Lincoln to hold these convictions:

> When I so pressingly urge a strict observance of the laws let me not be understood as saying there are no bad laws, or that grievances may not arise for the redress of which no legal provisions have been made. I mean to say no such thing. But I do mean to say that although bad laws, if they exist, should be repealed as soon as possible, still while they continue in force, for the sake of example, they should be religiously observed.

The more a society expresses a true democratic spirit, the more it relies on shared respect for law, rather than coercive force, to uphold its ideals. In a dictatorship or totalitarian society, the law of the ruling class is imposed by force. Citizens adhere to the law out of fear. To make a democracy a possibility in a society, a deep trust in and allegiance to law is indispensable.

During the time of the civil rights movement, a strong case was made for civil disobedience as a tactic for changing unjust laws. In retrospect, it may seem that such a strategy was justifiable, and achieved certain goals. But at the time, I found it very difficult to condone any form of disobedience to law as a means of trying to change the law, despite my strong moral identification with the motives of the civil rights movement. I reasoned then that I could countenance such action in a thoroughly totalitarian society where the options for change through the process of the law were nearly nonexistent. But in our society, despite the tragic inequities and terrible injustice that existed, I found it troublesome that the law would be purposefully disobeyed as part of the strategy for reforming the law. If a civil rights bill was passed, wouldn't unsympathetic whites then feel justified in disobeying its provisions? These were some of my thoughts when I began to serve my first term in the U.S. Senate.

Choosing to disobey certain laws because one believes them to be unjust puts one beyond the law. There is a kind of moral superiority that is established. Someone has to select which laws are worthy and just enough to be obeyed and which are not. When we are dealing with clearly moral issues, such as was the case with the civil rights movement, it may seem feasible and appropriate, for many reasons, to follow this course of action. It can be argued, after all, that the blatant injustice of certain laws affecting blacks was painfully clear, and that to abide by those laws was to uphold and sustain injustice. The principle applied was that certain laws could be disobeyed for overriding moral considerations.

But let us see what happens when that principle is applied to other spheres of our national life. The scandal of the Watergate affair, it seems to me, provides a revealing and frightening case in point. For after all, was not this what went on in the minds of those in the Nixon administration allegedly involved in severe breaches of the law? Didn't they rationalize, to themselves, that the overriding moral consideration of reelecting the President, and saving the country from his opponent, justified the disobedience of certain laws? Didn't they choose which laws they should obey, and which laws they should overlook and ignore? Didn't they assume a sense of moral superiority that put them beyond the law?

I realize that there are some respects in which this analogy breaks down. Those in the civil rights movement practicing civil disobedience were fully prepared to acknowledge their acts, and accept the legal consequences. That is a trait painfully absent from any of those allegedly involved in the Watergate affair. Further, civil disobedience in moral issues like the civil rights movement and the antiwar movement frequently were acts of conscience clearly motivated by deep religious convictions, rather than by zealous political ambitions. It is undeniable, though, that the Watergate scandal illustrates the terrifying consequences that can ensue when persons decide that they can place themselves beyond the rule of law, and then follow that practice to ultimate extremes.

The Watergate case is such an utterly devastating scandal because it strikes at the very core of a democracy's existence— trust in the sanctity of law. This is the trust that has been so grossly violated, according to the allegations, by the very men charged with protecting and preserving that trust on behalf of all people. When those in the leadership of government sacrifice laws like pawns in their quest for power, then the people wonder why they should sustain their faith in government by law.

In this all, we see the gravity, the risk, and the potential danger of assuming that a citizen may have justification for choosing to disobey the obligations of law at some point. Regardless of how high and pure the motives, and how reprehensible the law, any decision to ignore the mandate of law may have the potential of imperiling a democracy's basic hope and strength—the shared trust in the law's efficacy to govern.

What then does one say about the dictates of conscience? Is the law never to be breached? When society's mandates and the individual's convictions are placed in fundamental conflict, do society's obligations also demand individual sacrifice?

And is the law the ultimate end, in and of itself, or does it stand under some accountability to the fundamental God-given rights of man?

Any individual's answer to such probing will come from his deep, inner convictions. Each person must ask himself whether or not he is ever answerable to any convictions, or to his conscience, or to his God, before he is obliged to the laws of his country.

The law, of course, is to be the guarantee of our freedom of conscience, belief and conviction. Yet we know that we have been subject to laws which would have directly forced individuals to violate their conscience, and forsake their religious convictions. This is an inescapable reality.

I can only answer this question in intensely personal terms, in the light of my deeply felt convictions.

There is an ultimate claim on my life, and that is the claim of Christ, for I am a follower of his. To put this more theologically, I am committed to the Lordship of Jesus Christ in my life. As such, he is the source of my ultimate authority and allegiance. All other commitments, demands and obligations are potentially subject to this focal point in my life.

Then I must ask, do the duties of a Christian and the law of the state ever come into direct conflict? The answer to that will still be highly individualistic. It is instructive, however, to place this question in a theological and a historical perspective.

Basically, the Christian owes obedience to the state insofar as this does not involve disobedience to God. When the claims of each come into direct conflict, the Christian has but one choice, and that is to obey God rather than Caesar.

Historically, it is worth noting early examples of conflicting demands from the state and from religious faith. The first Christians in the early church gave their primary allegiance to Christ's kingdom, rather than to the empire of Rome. Early Christians refrained from giving oaths of allegiance to the emperor and the empire, and refused to join the Roman army. They did not even participate in the Roman court system, which they thought to be unjust.

The state's response was one of harsh repression. The case of Maximilian, a young Christian in the third century, is one of several recorded in history. Maximilian appeared before an African proconsul named Dion for induction into the Roman army. Maximilian refused induction simply stating, "I cannot serve for I am a Christian." Dion replied, "Get into the service or it will cost you your life." Maximilian's last remark was, "I do this age no war service, but I do war service for my God." He was executed March 12, A.D. 295. His father returned home in pride of his son's unbending loyalty to God. Historians report that there were many cases like this which probably led to the massive persecution of Christians in A.D. 303.

Tertullian, a third-century Christian father, explained the thinking of such early Christians by asking, "If we are to love our enemies, whom have we to hate? Who then can suffer injury at our hand?" There is record that the Roman official Celsus continually insisted that Christians fulfill their duty to the king. He stated that if everybody followed their ethic of nonresistance, the empire would be ruined. Origen, another learned father of the early church, specifically rebutted the position of Celsus by saying, "We have come in accordance with the council of Jesus to cut down our arrogant swords of arguments into plowshares, and we convert into sickles the spears we formerly used in fighting, for we no longer take swords against a nation nor do we learn any more to make war, having become sons of peace for the sake of Jesus who is our Lord."

This era of sharp conflict between the state and the conscience of Christians was ended by the "conversion" of Constantine in the fourth century. As a result of that act, the Empire was "Christianized," and the clergy received major benefits in exchange for their allegiance to the state. Thus, the church embarked on a course that allied it in support of political power. In fact, after Constantine's conversion, whole Roman legions were marched through rivers to be baptized before they were sent off to battle.

The alliance between church and state that developed over the ensuing centuries erased most of the memory of the church's earliest history, and blurred the biblical understanding of the relationship between Caesar and God. The effects of this history are plainly evident still today as our own government and others attempt to use a "civil religion" to sanctify and justify their purposes.

Recently, however, there has been an increased awareness in the church of the potential conflict between certain demands imposed by political powers and the dictates of one's faith. Personally, I know cases where the conscience of a Christian has put him in tension with the requirements of the state.

This, then, is how I, as one individual person, think about the relationship between conscience and the law. Rather than give an abstract analysis of such a classical question, I have tried to explain my personal credo, how it shapes my conscience, and how I would face in my own life a contradictory demand between my deepest personal convictions and obligations of the law.

As one individual, I have to give my first and ultimate loyalty to my Christian faith. Out of this faith evolves the character of my conscience. I recognize in my own life the ultimacy of the urgings of that conscience.

If I acknowledge the primacy of conscience in my own life, then I certainly must accept and make provision for the same in lives of others.

Naturally, I realize that the conscience of another may be shaped by forces and beliefs completely different from my own. In describing how my personal Christian faith molds my convictions and has a final claim on my allegiance, I do not mean to convey that this is the only way conscience can make a legitimate, ultimate claim on one's obedience. Other individuals may have totally different views of religion. They may even hold to no specifically religious views at all, and may have no belief in a Supreme Being. Nevertheless, their convictions on matters of conscience can be just as ultimate for their lives, and are just as inviolate. This principle was upheld by the Supreme Court in its decision that belief in a Supreme Being was not essential to establish one's status as a conscientious objector to all war.

Any potential case where conscience may seem to entail a conflict with the law must be regarded with the gravest care—even with "fear and trembling." Further, the instances where this may be a possibility must involve only those laws which in and of themselves impose clear violations of more basic moral law and of fundamental human rights. This can be soundly argued to be the case with Jim Crow laws, fugitive slave laws, discrimination statutes, and the draft law. The conflict of conscience is created in such instances as these precisely because adhering to the specific law abrogates conscience.

The case of the Watergate scandal, for example, is decisively different in this regard. There, laws were violated not because they were, in and of themselves, an imposition on conscience, but simply because they stood in the way of achieving some end thought to be worthy—in this case, the reelection of President Nixon. Thus, it was determined that the end justified the means, so illegal means were condoned. No specific law was thought to violate conscience and therefore had to be questioned, or resisted. Rather, laws in general were seen as expendable in the pursuit of political aims. It was this attitude of being above the law—law which was regarded as legitimate and binding for all others—that constituted such a scandalous assault on the rule and sancitity of law.

Thus, there are crucial distinctions to be made even when we acknowledge that conscience may have a claim over the law. That never justifies an arrogant attitude toward the law. Rather, it takes all law with utter seriousness by holding it accountable to the law of conscience and morality. Liberty of conscience must be an ultimate value in a free society. When the law trespasses upon that liberty, it imperils the nation's most basic foundation and strength.

Chief Justice Harlan Fiske Stone eloquently made this point in 1919.

> The ultimate test of the course of action which the state should adopt will of course be the test of its own self-preservation; but with this limitation, at least in those countries where the political theory contains that the utimate end of the state is the highest good of its citizens, both morals and sound policy require that the state should not violate the conscience of the individual. All our history gives confirmation to the view that liberty of conscience has a moral and social value which makes it worthy of preservation at the hands of the state. So deep in its significance and vital, indeed, is it to the integrity of man's moral and spiritual nature that nothing short of the self-preservation of the state should warrant its violation; and it may well be questioned whether the state which preserves its life by a settled policy of violation of the conscience of the individual will not in fact ultimately lose it by the process.

Here, then, is the total context from which I approach the question of amnesty. The war was immoral, and the draft a violation of basic rights. I am utterly committed to upholding the sanctity of the law. Nevertheless, I acknowledge that there may be cases where allegiance to conscience takes precedence over a law's requirements.

The initial question to be addressed in considering amnesty, regardless of one's views of the war, is whether the law has in fact made sufficient provision for respecting individual conscience. A system does exist, after all, exempting a citizen who proves himself to be a conscientious objector to all war from military service. Further, a procedure for being discharged from the military for those same grounds also has been in effect. When we review how these provisions have actually operated, however, it seems clear that they have been far from sufficient in respecting the liberty of conscience.

First of all, the only grounds for such objection are that one is opposed to all war or that one is a committed pacifist. But, clearly, one could be opposed for the deepest reasons of conscience to the Vietnam war without taking a totally consistent pacifist position; in fact, one could even believe that every other war in our history has been just, rightly demanding the sacrifice of its citizens. There are thousands of individuals whose conscience places themselves in opposition to the Vietnam war, but not to all war, and who, therefore, were liable to the draft laws.

Secondly, even if one was a consistent conscientious objector, one frequently had to go through an arduous, and often inequitable, process to prove the integrity of one's convictions. For one who had grown up in the tradition of a pacifist church, gaining such a status was routine. But for one who came to such convictions individually, and especially if one did so after reaching the age of eighteen and registering for the draft, it was necessary to convince others beyond a shadow of a doubt that one's convictions were valid. With a draft board facing quotas to fill, and perhaps comprised of members who were less than sympathetic to those seeking changes in their draft status, there was no certainty that justice would be insured in each case.

The historical record makes it manifest that the operation of the law fell far short of making sufficient allowance for the liberty of conscience. Therefore, we must determine how the law can be modified to make provision for its past inadequacies, insuring a greater measure of liberty and justice for all. This would be the purpose of any form of amnesty.

It is useful first to review the evolution of various forms of amnesty in our nation's history.

One distinctive feature of the U.S. Constitution is that it grants the power of pardon, and implicitly, amnesty, to the Executive rather than the legislature. Article II, Section 2 states that the "President . . . shall have Power to grant Reprieves and Pardons for Offenses against the United States, except in Cases of Impeachment." This power is not granted exclusively to the President, however, and Congress has taken a role in providing amnesties or pardons in several instances, most especially during and after the Civil War. The role was sanctioned by the Supreme Court in 1896, when the Court held that the President did not have sole authority in this area.

On July 10, 1795 President Washington granted a "full, free and entire pardon" to the insurrectionists in the Whiskey Rebellion, this being the first grant of amnesty or pardon under the new Constitution. The rebels, who had found it much easier to bring corn liquor to market than corn grain, and had resisted a federal excise tax on distilled spirits by attacking the home of the local tax collector, had only to promise they would not resist again the tax laws or other laws of the United States in order to receive pardon. In informing Congress of his action, President Washington made a statement that is well worth remembering today:

> For though I shall always think it a sacred duty to
> exercise with firmness and energy the constitutional

powers with which I am vested, yet my personal feeling
is to mingle in the operations of the Government every
degree of moderation and tenderness which the national
justice, dignity and safety may permit.

Five years later, on May 20, 1800, President Adams
granted a full pardon to the insurrectionists who had opposed
property tax laws in Pennsylvania. Apparently no conditions
were attached.

Beginning in 1807, and lasting through 1814, there was a
series of Presidential pardons granted to deserters from the army
who surrendered themselves in four months and returned to
duty. No other qualifications were provided.

President Jackson made further exceptions to a general
pardon for deserters in 1830, after Congress had repealed the
death penalty for peacetime desertion. Jackson stipulated that
those in confinement were to be released and returned to duty,
while those at large and under a sentence of death were to be
discharged and never allowed to serve again. As a former soldier
himself, Jackson would be expected to be more stern with deserters than his civilian predecessors.

The Civil War and its aftermath prompted more amnesties
and pardons than any other period in American history hereto-
fore, beginning with President Lincoln's pardon in 1862 of political prisoners in military custody jailed at the outset of the conflict. The sole requirement for release was an assurance that the
prisoners would "render no aid or comfort to the enemies in
hostility to the United States." A special commission was created
to review the cases of those held by state authorities.

Congress began to take a part in the granting of amnesties
and pardons with the passage of the Confiscation Law of 1862,
legislation authorizing the President to extend pardon and amnesty on terms he deemed expedient to those participating in the
rebellion. It is interesting to note that Lincoln acknowledged
this act in subsequent proclamations, but never claimed it was

his sole authority for granting amnesty. From 1862 on, with and without Congressional resolutions, Lincoln granted several pardons to deserters, with a variety of conditions, primarily a requirement that deserters return to duty within a specified time and serve so long as the commander deemed it beneficial.

On December 8, 1863, Lincoln issued a proclamation of pardon that is indicative of his desire for reconciliation rather than retribution:

> Whereas it is now desired by some persons heretofore engaged in said rebellion to resume their allegiance to the United States and to reinaugurate loyal State governments . . . a full pardon is hereby granted to them and each of them, with restoration of all rights of property, except as to slaves and in property cases where rights of third parties shall have intervened . . .

Although Lincoln found it necessary to modify this sweeping pardon in later years, this modification was due more to abuses by its recipients than to any desire to narrow the intent.

President Andrew Johnson did his best to continue Lincoln's policy of reconciliation with the South, despite increasing opposition from the Congress. On May 29, 1865, Johnson issued a "Proclamation of Amnesty and Reconstruction," which granted full pardon to all former Confederates (except certain leaders) who took an oath of allegiance to the United States. This roused the ire of Congress, which repealed that portion of the Confiscation Law that gave the President discretionary power to set the terms for amnesty and pardon. Johnson ignored this action, and continued to issue proclamations extending the pardon until on December 25, 1868, he granted full pardon and amnesty to "all persons engaged in the late rebellion," with no exceptions.

Congress reacted with a report by the Senate Judiciary Committee declaring Johnson's amnesty unconstitutional. Although no action was taken on the report, Congress became more attentive to the issue of amnesty and relief from political disability. Ratification of the Fourteenth Amendment in 1868, however, gave the Congress specific authority to remove prohibitions against the holding of state or federal office by participants in the rebellion against the United States.

Having acquired the authority to do so, Congress gradually became more lenient in granting amnesty, but not until 1898 was a universal amnesty bill passed for all those involved in the Civil War, and by that time most of those affected had died.

In the first two decades of the twentieth century, two Presidential amnesties were granted, for the Philippine Insurrection and to relieve the effects of a Supreme Court ruling. In 1924, President Coolidge granted amnesty and restored citizenship to approximately one hundred men who had deserted after the World War I armistice and lost their citizenship under a 1912 law. In 1933, President Roosevelt granted amnesty and citizenship to violators of draft and espionage laws who had completed their sentences.

Of more relevance to us today is the action taken on amnesty after World War II. By an Executive Order on December 23, 1946, President Truman created the President's Amnesty Board to review the cases of 15,805 violators of the Selective Service Act of 1940. In its report of December 1947, the Board recommended amnesty for 1,523 of these offenders, in addition to 618 previously pardoned by Presidential proclamation and 900 who had entered the armed forces. Truman pardoned all men on December 23, 1947.

On December 24, 1952, President Truman issued two proclamations of pardon. The first pardoned ex-convicts who had served not less than one year in the Korean War; the second amnestied all those who had deserted between July 14, 1945 and June 25, 1950 and had been court-martialed or dishonorably discharged, or both. There is no record of any presidential pardon or amnesty for draft violators or deserters after 1952.

This history reveals that amnesty for those guilty or allegedly guilty of criminal acts in opposition to the Vietnam war, while not entirely without precedent, would be at the least unusual in its scope and application. Yet, the war itself was without historical precedent as a major conflict never declared by the Congress, and never winning the unified backing of the population as being just and essential for our country.

As of September 1, 1971, 30,259 deserters from the armed forces were still at large. Figures for draft evaders are not as precise, since the Selective Service System lacks any centralized record-keeping mechanism. Some indication can be gained from Justice Department figures on cases of draft law violations. As of June 29, 1973, 204,000 alleged violations of the Military Selective Service Act had been reported to the U.S. Attorney for FBI investigation and possible indictment by the Justice Department, for the period of fiscal years 1963-1972. Indictments were filed in approximately 25,500 of these cases, 10,350 of which were concluded by trial, with convictions obtained in 8,100. Since its renewal in 1963, approximately 3,900 men have served sentences for violation of the Military Selective Service Act, and approximately 250 were in custody as of March 31, 1973. Furthermore, the Justice Department estimated that as of June 29, 1973 there were 4,670 fugitives against whom federal arrest warrants were outstanding, 2,900 of whom were believed to be in Canada and 610 in other foreign countries; the whereabouts of the balance is unknown.

When the number of men serving sentences for desertion, performing alternate service as conscientious objectors in the I-O or I-A-O classifications, and not yet reported as violators by the Selective Service System are added to these figures, the total number of men who could be considered for amnesty is far greater than that we have previously encountered, except for Confederates receiving amnesty after the Civil War. And there are differences between the two wars which make amnesty in the present case more difficult.

Restoration of the Union, Lincoln's most cherished goal, could hardly have been achieved had the victors attempted to prosecute and imprison all the rebels. They represented a far greater percentage of the total population than do the Vietnam resisters, and their imprisonment would have crippled the rebuilding and expansion of the nation after the war. Therefore, amnesty was clearly in the national interest. Furthermore, the Vietnam resisters are seen as men who refused to fight against a foreign enemy, however unclear the precise identity of that enemy may have been. Despite the bitterness of the Civil War, there was always a sense that those in the seceded states were, after all, Americans. It may have been more understandable, then, that there were many who were reluctant to fight for the sake of preserving a political entity.

Nevertheless, the comparison with the Civil War is informative, for it suggests that the Vietnam war has been as divisive as the one which literally tore this country asunder. There is much to be learned, therefore, from Lincoln's understanding of the need for reconstruction and reconciliation, an understanding that prompted his and Johnson's proclamations of pardon and amnesty. Historians have long since concluded that the "radical Republicans" and others who rejected this understanding and imposed a retributive Reconstruction aggravated the wounds of war rather than healed them.

There are four groups of Vietnam war resisters to be considered for amnesty or pardon: (1) those who are presently in prison or who have served sentences for draft resistance; (2) those who have allegedly violated the provisions of the Military Selective Service Act and are still at large, under indictment, or in custody; (3) conscientious objectors in the I-O and I-A-O classifications who are presently performing or have performed alternate service, including military duty as noncombatants;

(4) those who have deserted the armed forces for genuine reasons of conscience.

In considering how to act in each of these circumstances, two preeminent principles must be borne in mind. First, did the individual, acting out of authentic conscience, choose to accept the full legal consequences of his action? We must uphold the principle that those who act in conscience against the law should be expected to be accountable for the consequences of that act. Second, did that act of conscience infringe upon or affect the rights of others? We must recognize that conscience cannot absolve one's responsibility for jeopardizing the rights of others, if this is a consequence. With these principles in mind, let me suggest a procedure for considering amnesty in the case of each of the four groups involved.

I

Draft resisters who are presently in jail should be granted amnesty by immediate release, expungement of record, and restoration of the full rights of citizenship. Those who have served sentences should be granted amnesty by expungement of record and restoration of rights. Finally, those who have been convicted but not yet sentenced should be released from custody, have the convictions set aside, and the record expunged. This amnesty should apply only to those guilty of failing to report for or refusing induction, and should not extend to acts involving the destruction of government property or Selective Service records, or harm to individuals. Amnesty in this and all other cases is to be provided only for those acts which did not involve infringement against other persons or property. Those offenses should remain within the usual jurisdiction of the criminal justice system.

For some of these men the Selective Service System and the draft were seen as totalitarian institutions that had no place in a society professing devotion to the cause of "life, liberty and the pursuit of happiness." Others may have been refused conscientious objector status because their objection was to the immorality of the Vietnam war alone, rather than to war in all its forms. My proposal of amnesty for these men is not based solely on my personal sympathy for their convictions. Whatever their reasons for refusing induction, these men accepted the political and social responsibility of adherence to the law, and faced the consequences of violating it. It is because of this willingness to be held accountable for their acts, in addition to their moral opposition of conscience to the war and the draft, that I would grant them full amnesty.

Regardless of what we may believe about the rightness or wrongness of the war, we all can share a basic and deep respect for those who acted in conscience and were fully prepared to go to prison, remaining under the constraints of the law, for their convictions. The integrity of their convictions cannot be questioned. Because of regard for the liberty of conscience these men should be given a complete and unconditional amnesty.

II

We must recognize that draft evaders have not accepted the full responsibility for their acts of resistance. These men choose to deny the obligation to their communities and cut off their relationship and opportunities of service to their fellow citizens. No doubt most chose exile out of deep moral commitment, for which we should have respect, and no doubt many have suffered in that exile, for which we should have compassion. But this does not mean we can blindly endorse their violation of the law. If only the deepest convictions of conscience can override obedience to the law, then those convictions can be expected to be strong enough to endure the consequences of the acts they compel.

Yet, provision for amnesty should be made possible for those who acted in genuine conscientious objection to the Vietnam war, even with the recognition that they did not live by all the legal consequences of that conviction. The choice to avoid being imprisoned for convictions of conscience is at least understandable. That should not preclude their ability to return to their country.

By the same token, it would seem fair and just to provide a means for judging the authenticity of their convictions. To accomplish this all, I would suggest the following procedure.

All indictments, arrest warrants and FBI investigations concerning draft evaders should be suspended, and those in custody released, pending review of their cases. Amnesty Appeal Councils should be established, one in each circuit of the U.S. Court of Appeals, in order to attempt an even distribution of the case load. The chief judge of each circuit should appoint three civilians from within the circuit to serve as members of the Council, none of whom shall have served on state or local draft boards or in the Selective Service System. Each Council should have access to all Selective Service and Justice Department records concerning the cases to be reviewed, and the records should be referred to the appropriate Council within a certain specified time. Each Council should have a staff adequate to assist in the review.

The Selective Service System, if still extant, and the Justice Department would have the opportunity to grant amnesty on their own initiative by deferring to the appropriate Council only those cases which they wish to contest. Should the Selective Service System or Justice Department choose not to contest a particular case, it should be dropped with no threat of further prosecution, arrest or investigation, and the record expunged. It is apparent from the figures cited earlier on Justice Department action on Selective Service cases that the Justice Department has already exercised this option by gaining indictments in a little more than 10% of the reported violations.

This structure roughly parallels that of the Truman Amnesty Review Board, although there are some differences. The far greater case load requires several Amnesty Appeal Councils, but each would have a smaller case load than the Truman Board. Appointment by the chief judge of the appeals circuit would emphasize the goal of justice rather than retribution, and remove the amnesty process from the political arena in which the Congress and the President so fiercely fought over the merits of the Vietnam war. Since the Amnesty Appeal Council would be empowered to recognize the legitimacy of "selective" conscientious objector status, it would better serve the interests of justice to bar from membership those who could not or would not grant such status during the war.

As soon as possible after the deadline for referral of cases to the Amnesty Appeal Councils, there should be a publication of the names of all those individuals whose cases are to be considered, and where the cases will be heard. Hearings should begin as soon as possible after this public announcement. Draft evaders should have ninety days to report to the Council in their district, adequate time to allow them to return from their exile. Immunity from arrest should be given during this time, and extended after the evader has reported to the Council. If the individual fails to report, he should not be considered for amnesty, since it will be assumed that he has chosen to remain outside the United States. Upon reporting to the Council, the evader should be given a date to appear for a hearing of his case.

At that hearing, the Council should hear all evidence from the individual and his supporters on his claim of conscientious objection to the Vietnam war. The Council should take care to remember that the conscientious objection need not be one against war in any form, but only against the Vietnam war; and that amnesty shall be granted in all such cases.

I realize this is a departure from the usual procedure for conscientious objection established by the Selective Service System, but there are good reasons for this distinction.

I have already indicated my beliefs about the immorality of the Vietnam war. Obviously all Americans do not share this conclusion, yet it is true that a majority of Americans came to see the war in some sense as a mistake, even while it was still going on. This lack of support for a war effort is entirely unprecedented in American history. It is hardly surprising, therefore, that many men could find themselves opposed to it on conscientious grounds, and yet not be conscientious objectors to war in any form.

We should remember that the Vietnam war is the only war these men have ever known—most were only children when it began. Those of us, like me, who can remember other wars cannot blithely pretend that this one was no different in its clarity of purpose, its horrors, or its divisive effect upon our country. To do so would be to insulate ourselves from its grim reality, and rob us of any chance to learn its lessons.

This war, unlike any other in memory, imposed burdens the conscience of many could not bear. Granting "selective" conscientious objector status as a basis for amnesty simply recognizes this fact.

I would further suggest that the Council not determine the authenticity of a claim to conscientious objection to the war solely on the individual's eloquence in substantiating that claim, nor necessarily on record of opposition to the war prior to his refusal of induction. Conscientious objector status has too often been an enclave of the educated, denied those whose convictions were no less deeply felt but somehow less persuasively presented.

Should the Council determine, after considering these factors, that the individual has a conscientious objection to the Vietnam war, then it should grant him amnesty through protection from all further prosecution, arrest or investigation for his act. If the Council should find that the individual does not have a conscientious objection to the Vietnam war, he should be given thirty days of immunity from arrest to allow him to leave the country if he so chooses. This immunity from arrest should not apply to any other violation of the law. Beyond thirty days, the individual would be liable to further prosecution for his act of resistance.

It should be remembered the Amnesty Review Councils will be considering only those cases that are contested by the Justice Department. Thus, amnesty would be automatically extended to all other cases where the Justice Department, in light of the criteria established for the possible amnesty, offers no objection.

In no case should amnesty be granted for acts involving damage to other persons or property. This amnesty is intended only for those whose opposition to the war did not entail violations of the rights of others.

The thrust of this proposal is to allow us to be as generous as possible without impugning justice. Amnesty is to serve the spirit of reconciliation, and reconciliation demands that we not be intractable and legalistic.

The intention of the Councils is to promote such a spirit, while enabling the individual attention to cases that is a reasonable expectation in a society based on law. Amnesty does not mean forgiveness. It means forgetting. The procedure I have outlined for those in exile would be a responsible manner for society to judge carefully the authenticity of offenses of conscience, and allow them to be legitimately erased from culpability.

III

The inclusion of conscientious objectors in the I-O and

I-A-O classifications in an amnesty proposal may seem inappropriate. Technically, these men cannot be granted amnesty, for they have committed no crime. According to Selective Service rules governing alternate service, however, these men have had their normal lives interrupted in some of the same ways as those drafted into the military. Those conscientious objectors presently performing civilian alternate service or serving as noncombatants in the military, therefore, should be immediately relieved of all further obligations to service. They may, of course, voluntarily continue this service and its responsibilities.

For those conscientious objectors who have completed two years of service, there is the possibility of G.I. benefits. U.S. district courts in Massachusetts and California have recently delivered conflicting opinions on this matter, and the cases are likely to come before the Supreme Court for final resolution. Since Selective Service regulations have also required that alternate service impose a hardship comparable to that of military life and be service in the national interest, it is my personal hope that the Court will decide to grant these benefits to conscientious objectors who performed such alternate service, as required by law.

IV

The question of amnesty for deserters is particularly difficult. To begin with, deserters are subject to the Uniform Code of Military Justice, violations of which are not ordinarily in the jurisdiction of the Justice Department or the federal courts. But this is not an insurmountable problem. The Code is, after all, part of the federal body of statutes that is proposed and passed by Congress, and civilian control of the military remains a strong American tradition. It is the intensity of feelings that makes amnesty for deserters such a sensitive issue.

Deserters are generally regarded as cowards who betrayed their comrades and left them at the mercy of the enemy. Those who desert under fire, it is said, should be shot. Even people who can unhesitatingly support unconditional amnesty for draft evaders often pull up short at the prospect of amnesty for deserters, and for good reason.

We should remember, however, that amnesty for deserters is not without precedent. As noted earlier, there have been several amnesties for deserters in our history. In fact, of the thirty-five amnesties or pardons in American history, ten of them were granted to deserters. It is true that most of these amnesties were dependent upon the offender's return to duty, a condition which might not be logical in the present situation, for most of these men deserted because they no longer wished to serve in the military. Forcing them to return as a condition for amnesty makes the military service punitive, and insults the concept of honorable military duty.

It is also true that the number of the deserters who could be considered for amnesty is greater than in earlier instances. But again, this is no more unprecedented than the war itself. One of the more remarkable scenes from the television coverage of the war was the sight of men explaining why they had refused to obey orders to participate in the Cambodian invasion. That scene and the immediacy of its presence in our homes certainly underlined the fact that this was no ordinary war.

Even the extraordinary circumstances of this war, however, cannot excuse desertion when it threatens the lives of others. In a military group under fire, the lives of all depend upon the actions of each. At that point, the consequences of an individual's act are no longer his to bear alone. Other lives may hang in the balance. Desertion in this situation is criminal, and should be treated as such.

There are times, however, when desertion does not imperil

the lives of others. It may pose an inconvenience, but it does not directly pose any threat whatsoever. It is these desertions which I believe could be reviewed for amnesty.

To do so, I would suggest that the President appoint a six-member board to review all cases of desertion presented it by the armed services by a specific date. Three board members should be civilians, and three should be from the military. As with the procedure for evaders, the respective branch of the service would be able to grant its own form of amnesty on its own initiative by deciding not to contest the case. Should the service not refer the case to the board, it should grant a general discharge, with forfeiture of pay from the date of desertion.

In reviewing the cases presented it, the board should base its determination on two factors: the individual's conscientious objection to the Vietnam war; and the conditions under which he deserted, with particular attention to the threat his desertion posed to the lives of others. The individual would not be required to be present at the hearing, nor should his absence be weighed against him, but his presence would obviously be beneficial to his case. The board should be empowered to grant discharges from general to dishonorable, or return the case to the respective service with recommendations as to further disposition. As Commander-in-Chief, the President would be able to grant amnesty to any and all he deemed proper, and appeals of the board's decision could be made to him. In no case, however, should this amnesty be granted for acts of violence against persons or property.

There are those who would argue that these men made their decision to accept military service, and they should always have to live with the obligations imposed by that decision. But for many of the men who served during the Vietnam war era, the military was the lesser of several evils when compared to jail or self-imposed exile for draft refusal. To refuse amnesty for these men and those who volunteered because they did not come to oppose the war until they actually confronted it, while extending it to those who came to this realization earlier and were articulate enough to establish their position or were able to flee the country, would be to exacerbate existing injustices in our land. That simply would not be fair or just to all concerned. The procedure suggested here fully reflects the more complex difficulties encountered by those who have deserted. It totally recognizes their abridgment of serious obligations, and the criminal culpability that is entailed. Yet, it provides the flexibility necessary if the standard of justice regarding the dictates of conscience are to be extended to all.

Many proposals of amnesty for draft evaders have included a provision for compulsory national service, under the assumption that these men owe the state some years of their lives. I agree that these men have an obligation to discharge, but it is to their communities, and their fellow citizens. A civilian draft would be no less onerous than military conscription. I would therefore strongly encourage, but not legally require, these men to serve in any federal, state or local volunteer agency that is seeking to meet the needs of others and improve their communication. The spirit of reconciliation that prompts us to grant amnesty to these men should also spur them to service.

The reconciliation this proposal for amnesty seeks could be jeopardized if it is enacted prematurely. Yet it is time to present proposals like this one and discuss them in an atmosphere free of inflammatory rhetoric. The war may have ended in Southeast Asia, but it continues in the division of our people. Reconciliation through amnesty can restore our community, so that altogether we may begin to learn the lessons of the war.

Self-analysis is always more difficult than either self-hatred or self-righteousness; that is just as true for the nation as it is for the individual. As a people, I believe we must try to understand what the Vietnam war has put us through, and where we are going. This is not merely a corporate exercise, but should involve individual, highly personal reflection for each of us. I am reminded of the words of Carl Jung, who wrote:

> This war has pitilessly revealed to civilized man that he is still a barbarian, and has at the same time shown what an iron scourge lies in store for him if ever again he should be tempted to make his neighbor responsible for his own evil qualities. The psychology of the individual is reflected in the psychology of the Nation. What the nation does is done also by the individual, and so long as the individual continues to do it, the Nation will do likewise. Only a change in the attitude of the individual can initiate a change in psychology of the Nation.

Our nation's foremost need is the recovery of a relevant moral conscience. Ultimately, that can only be done through individuals, not by the state. But the state exists to serve the people. Its highest calling is to ensure the individual's freedom to determine the dictates of his conscience, and act upon them. At this time in our history it is more crucial than ever for us to guarantee that freedom.

This must begin by healing the wounds that have taken root within our own hearts, and then reconciling ourselves to each other. That will build the climate for a spirit of reconciliation to reign, ending the war that has raged not only beyond our land, but within it.